Evangelical
Is Not Enough

Thomas Howard

THOMAS NELSON PUBLISHERS
Nashville • Camden • New York

Published in Nashville, Tennessee, by Thomas Nelson,
Inc. and distributed in Canada by Lawson Falle, Ltd.,
Cambridge, Ontario.

Printed in the United States of America.

Scripture quotations are from the King James Version of the Bible

Portions of Chapter 8 previously appeared in the author's book *The
Liturgy Explained* copyright © 1981 by Thomas Howard and are used with
the permission of the publisher Morehouse Barlow Co., Inc.

ISBN 0-8407-5372-1

Contents

1. Protestant and Evangelical: Understanding
   Ourselves   1
2. Spirit and Flesh: Sundered Forever or Reunited? ..   21
3. Christian Worship: Act or Experience?   41
4. Prayer: Random or Disciplined?   63
5. Hail, Blessed Virgin Mary: What Did the Angel
   Mean?   79
6. Ritual and Ceremony: A Dead Hand or the Liberty
   of the Spirit?   91
7. Table and Altar: Supper and Sacrament 105
8. The Eucharistic Liturgy: Diagram and Drama 115
9. The Liturgical Year: Redeeming the Time 131
10. Envoi 149
    For Further Reading 157
    Notes 159

Dedication

Dedications are ordinarily made to one person, sometimes two. I would like to break with that convention in this one instance and dedicate my book to the following multitude. Some of them would not at all want their names associated with a single one of the ideas expressed in the book, and I absolve them entirely. Remember, this is only a dedication, not a board of reference.

There are some mightily strange bedfellows here, but all share at least two things. First, all of them confess our Lord Jesus Christ with a clarity and fidelity that is more than heartening to a fellow-Christian, and all are serious about being faithful to the ancient Faith, which He committed to His apostles and which has been witnessed to by those apostles, and by martyrs, confessors, doctors, widows, virgins, and all the great company of the faithful for two thousand years now. Second, whether they themselves know it or not (and many of them have never heard of me, and some are dead), I owe each one some debt in the Faith.

I would like, then, to make this dedication:

To John Henry Newman, Ronald Knox, Maurice Zundel,
and Romano Guardini: my Roman Catholic tutors.

To Alexander Schmemann, Kallistos Ware, and Georges
Florovsky: my tutors in holy Orthodoxy.

To Lancelot Andrewes, George Herbert, Gregory Dix,
T. S. Eliot, C. S. Lewis, J. I. Packer, John Stott,
Mark Dyer, and Jeffrey Steenson:
Anglican witnesses to the Faith.

To my former students James Gurley, Harold Fickett,
John Skillen, Michael Barwell, and Dan Ohman:
they fill me with hope.

To Philip E. Howard, Jr., Joseph Bayly, David Wells,
Gerald Hawthorne, and the missionaries of the
China Inland Mission: these embody the evan-
gelical integrity I honor.

To the bishops of the Evangelical Orthodox Church: At
enormous cost they have staked everything for the sake of the
one, holy, catholic, and apostolic Church for which I pray
daily.

Evangelical
Is Not Enough

Protestant and Evangelical: Understanding Ourselves

My debt to Protestantism is incalculable. The Reformation was my tutor in the Faith. Since my pilgrimage has led me to ancient forms of Christian worship and discipline that find little place in ordinary Reformational piety and vision, I find myself mulling over just what Protestantism might be, in the effort to chart my own itinerary.

Who Are We?

What, exactly, is Protestantism's genius? Where is its center of gravity? Where does it stand in relation to the whole Church?

My own nurture took place in a particularly earnest and, to my mind, admirable sector of Protestantism, namely, evangelicalism. I have never come upon Christian believers of any ilk who exhibit more clearly than do the evangelicals the simplicity, earnestness, and purity of heart that the gospel asks of us.

The word *evangelical* is an ancient and noble one, but it has become somewhat rickety. It has too many meanings. In our own time it sprang into popular use with the presidency of Jimmy Carter, when anyone who claimed to be born again seemed to fall into the category. The press often used the word as a synonym for middle-class religion. On the other hand, there are the historic uses of the word. Originally it simply referred to the gospel. Late in time it referred to the union of Lu-

theran and Reformed churches in Prussia, or to European
Protestantism generally, or to the movement in the Church of
England that stressed personal conversion by faith in Christ's
atoning death. Names like George Whitefield and Charles Simeon loom large in this last connection.

The evangelicalism of which I speak differs slightly from
what one finds in Southern Baptist, Wesleyan, Pentecostal, or
Missouri Synod Lutheran circles, even though all of these may
lay claim to being evangelical in some sense.

I can best identify my own milieu by listing the following as
touchstones: Billy Graham; the Scofield Reference Bible;
Moody Bible Institute; Wheaton College; The China Inland
Mission; *The Sunday School Times*; Wycliffe Bible Transla-
tors; Youth For Christ; Young Life; Inter-Varsity Christian Fellowship; Campus Crusade for Christ; The Navigators;
Gordon-Conwell, Fuller, and Dallas Theological Seminaries;
and all the evangelical publishing houses such as Word, Flem-
ing H. Revell, and Tyndale, as well as the journals *Christianity
Today* and *Eternity*.

Everyone in my world could speak these names trippingly on
the tongue, even though there were many internecine differ-
ences. The theologians at Fuller Seminary, for example, would
not espouse the "dispensationalist" method of interpreting the
Bible taught at Dallas Seminary and plotted out in the Scofield
Bible.

A reader scanning this list will note that no church is mentioned. This is not without significance. While many small
evangelical denominations have been formed in the last eighty
years, the characteristic evangelical presence often lies in
"para-church" organizations or in independent local congregations with names like Grace Chapel or Calvary Baptist
Church. It is difficult for Christians with strong denomina-
tional loyalties, especially those with ethnic roots like the
Swedish Baptists, the Dutch Reformed, the German Luther-
ans, the Scottish Presbyterians, or the Plymouth Brethren, to
find the axis of evangelicalism. No city constitutes a Holy See,

for example—no Zurich, Geneva, Amsterdam, Edinburgh, or Prague. Nor is there any single founding father—no Jan Hus, Menno Simon, Alexander Campbell, John Calvin, Oecolampadius, or J. N. Darby. The words "interdenominational" and "nondenominational" are words of good omen, not bad omen, in this environment. We attached almost no importance to ancient historic credentials.

At bottom, though, one cannot distinguish evangelical teaching from traditional Christian orthodoxy. We could be counted on to embrace wholeheartedly all that is spelled out in the ancient creeds of the Church. There is nothing in the Apostles', Nicene, Chalcedonian, or Athanasian creeds that we would have jibbed at. We were stoutly among those who with Athanasius, "hold the Catholic Faith...whole and undefiled." In this sense we would have been more at home in the company of apostles, fathers, doctors, confessors, and the ancient tradition of catholic orthodoxy than among modern churchmen who look on the gospel as being shot through with legendary matter.

But there is something peculiar in this way of talking about evangelicalism. Our imagination did not run to creeds, fathers, doctors, tradition, or catholic orthodoxy. When it came to anchoring our faith, we cited texts from the New Testament and nothing else. We never said, "The Church teaches so and so." We were not thinking of the ancient Faith or of a long lineage of the faithful when we spoke of our beliefs. Yet there is perhaps nowhere in the world where ancient Christian belief is professed more candidly and vigorously than in evangelicalism.

Here, I think, lies the irony that has attended my pilgrimage. Have I moved or have I not?

I have certainly left nothing behind. I was taught, for example, that Jesus was born of a virgin. This meant that He did not have a human father. At the Annunciation the Holy Ghost brought about what ordinarily occurs at human conception. Something gynecological occurred. Evangelicalism teaches this; ancient catholic orthodoxy teaches this.

Over against this robust dogma lie all the delicate techniques for skirting the miracle. Early heretics came up with half a dozen artful formularies. Nineteenth-century modernists were frank enough to deny it flatly. More recent and oblique theologies bring literary criticism and the psychology of religion to bear on it, managing to keep the language of virgin birth alive while not actually believing a syllable of it. My own passage from childhood to adolescence to adulthood, and thence to approaching old age, has not obliged me to shift ground from what my Sunday school teachers taught me. They agreed with the fathers and doctors of the Church that the Virgin Birth happened in the real world before any early Christian piety went to work on the notion. Similarly, the Resurrection happened before any "Easter Faith" existed.

To this extent, then, I cannot be said to have traveled anywhere on my pilgrimage. I have no new light on things such as that claimed by Mormons, Christian Scientists, or Jehovah's Witnesses. Evangelicalism taught me all the major points taught by traditional orthodoxy. Against this stand all heresies, cults, and all forms of theological liberalism.

And yet the *flavor* of evangelicalism is very different from that of the traditional Church, which I have come to understand as being one, holy, catholic, and apostolic.

A Biblical Base

For one thing, we stressed the Bible alone as the touchstone for our doctrine, piety, and order. We distrusted the Roman Catholic and Eastern Orthodox emphasis on the Church as the guardian and teacher of Scripture, and even the Anglican formula of Scripture, tradition, and reason. There was even a slight but unmistakable difference between us and the Reformation itself with its cry of "*Sola Scriptura!*" It is so slight that perhaps the only way of identifying it is to say that if an evangelical ever visits a Lutheran or Reformed church, he does not find there quite the stress on each Christian's private spiritual life and devotional Bible reading that he finds in his native evangelicalism. To this extent evangelicalism would stand in Pietist and Wesleyan traditions and not quite in the classic Reformational heritage.

Evangelicalism's first and last instinct is to take the Bible at face value. What the Bible reports is true, we said. Moreover, the Bible stories are in some sense true *as they are told.* This holds not only for major doctrines like the Virgin Birth but for lesser stories as well. If the narrative tells of a rod that turns into a snake, or of a withered hand that suddenly becomes whole, then we are to take it as a true account of what happened in the real world. We are not reading a mere record of primitive faith. To reduce the Bible to forms that are routinely acceptable to modern categories is to subvert it. God has disclosed Himself not only in natural events like thunder and the whirlwind but also in signs and marvels, and it is these latter, especially, that attend and corroborate the drama of Redemption.

This stress on the Bible alone calls for a complicated vocabulary of "inerrancy" and "verbal inspiration" that has never marked Catholic and Orthodox theology, since these latter would look to the magisterium of the church, or to Holy Tradition, to keep the ancient Faith intact. The evangelicals, pinning everything as they do on the Bible alone, have had to devise formularies that will guard the text of Scripture while leaving room at the same time for discrepancies in the various Gospel accounts of Christ's life, for example. These formularies at times resemble the twelfth- and thirteenth-century attempts to chase down exactly what happens at the Mass, and it is very difficult to find phrases that avoid all the pitfalls. At the same time, it is probably fair to say that most of us did not concern ourselves with the fine points here any more than ordinary Catholics do with Thomistic formularies for the

Sacrament. Our assumption was that what we read in Genesis, Haggai, Luke, or Jude is true, trustworthy, important, and God's Word.

This sense in which evangelicalism is of one fabric with ancient orthodoxy and yet has an unmistakable texture of its own appears in other doctrinal emphases besides this focus on the Bible.

The Atonement

We laid great stress, for example, on Christ's atoning work and on his "vicarious, substitutionary" death. We believed nothing on this point that is not supported by traditional catholic dogma and Scripture. We all memorized texts like "Who his own self bare our sins in his own body on the tree" and "For [God] hath made him to be sin for us, who knew no sin; that we might be made the righteousness of God in him."[1] "He was wounded for our transgressions...the chastisement of our peace was upon him; and with his stripes we are healed" and "...the blood of Jesus Christ his Son cleanseth us from all sin."[2] These texts loomed large.

We knew that novels and Broadway plays retailed "the blood of the Lamb" as a sort of droll specialty of Salvationist and hillbilly religion. Judy Garland sang gaily, "Forget your troubles, come on, get happy, get ready for the Judgment Day ...wash your sins away in the tide." This treatment of the matter had the same ring to our ears as would the suggestion that everyone play tiddly-winks with the blessed Sacrament to a Catholic's ears. We could have appealed to the Roman Missal itself and to the Anglican *Book of Common Prayer* to show the world that a devout attitude towards Christ's blood is no specialty of hillbillies.

We were aware that "our" kind of preaching was what attracts huge numbers of converts. You cannot flag down busy modern people with a gospel that offers nothing but caring and sharing. Liberal Protestants are vexed when their churches dwindle, despite all their infinitely resourceful and energetic programs to update the gospel, while evangelical churches fill up and burst with converts. Millions of confessing Christians credit Billy Graham or Young Life or Campus Crusade with having brought them into the Faith by means of preaching what sounds for all the world like the gospel preached by Saint Peter at Pentecost or by Saint Paul at Athens, or for that matter, by our Lord Himself. It was He, after all, who said, "Ye must be born again."[3] Neither Billy Graham nor Billy Sunday, nor General Booth, nor even Chuck Colson made up that idea.

The Second Coming

As with our stress on the Bible and on faith in Christ's atoning death, we looked on the Second Coming as something of a specialty of our own. The doctrine is taught in the creeds, and, hence, all Christians are supposed to believe it. But many have only the dimmest notions about it. The liberals often appeared to suppose that things will gradually get better and better until at last, when we all have learned to be generous and thoughtful, a new Golden Age will arrive. The lion and lamb will lie down together, and all of us will beat our spears into pruning hooks.

That picture of the end is indeed scriptural, we said, but it is not going to come to pass by any gradual process whereby humanity improves its behavior. Things will probably get worse. We need only consult Jesus' own remarks about how history will go if we are not clear on that point. Evangelicals look, usually, for "the imminent, personal return of Christ in glory," basing this expectation on all of Christ's alarming words about how suddenly the Son of Man will come, and about watching, and about the cry, "Behold the bridegroom cometh!"[4] and about the Son of Man who will come in His glory with all the holy angels. Saint Paul also appeared to be on our side, with his teaching about the Lord Himself descending from heaven "with a shout, with the voice of the archangel, and with the trump of God."[5]

This language must not be watered down, we said. Surely it refers to the end of time as well as to how the Kingdom of God makes its way into the heart of man. The gospel pictures of sheep and goats, and of weeping and gnashing of teeth, and of God's saying, "Depart from me, ye cursed, into everlasting fire"[6] are all too violent to be ameliorated with oleaginous expressions of optimism.

Some evangelicals pasted bumper stickers on their cars in this connection, announcing the news that "Jesus Is Coming." Even though most of us drew the line short of this particular tactic, nevertheless we would all, if pressed, have urged that indeed it is an event that no mortal may ignore with anything approaching impunity.

The Judgment

The preacher regaling his quaking congregation with the blistering torments of hell is a comic figure in our time and is no more congenial to evangelicals than to anyone else. But we would have pointed out that this sort of preaching did not originate with stump preachers and tent evangelists. Dante drew grotesque pictures of hell's pains, and the Dominicans and Franciscans brought the art to a high degree of horror in their preaching. Seventeenth-century prelates like John Donne could dilate exquisitely on the clinical minutia of hell's agonies. They all took their cues from the apostles, who took theirs from Jesus. It was not Jonathan Edwards, after all, who invented the picture of the deathless worm gnawing damned souls. It was Jesus Christ Himself (cf. Mark 9:44–48).

In the face of dreadful texts like this, a liberal can say, "Oh, the text is corrupt," or "Jesus never said that," or "You must understand Jesus' first-century frame of mind." An evangelical, on the other hand, finds himself investing the words with something like their face value, no matter how crushing they may sound or how revolting to all his human instincts. The drama must include all the horrors somehow—real evil and real free will and hence real perdition, as well as the lilies of the field. Otherwise the thick darkness that shrouds the Passion of our Lord is not so thick after all. If the gospel says nothing more than that we should all try to be amiable, then there is a great deal of smoke and dust in the drama that ought long since to have been cleared away so that we could have been left with the gentle story that it really is.

Witnessing and Missions

Because of evangelicalism's zeal to get people saved, we developed what might be called a "task-force" strategy. We mobilized to carry the gospel to every conceivable cranny of the human endeavor: to the jungle, the steppes, and out of the way aboriginal islands; but also to skid row derelicts, Washington's social elite, prep school students, neighborhood children, military officers and enlisted men, doctors, businessmen, university students and faculties, Jews, and strangers on airplanes.

To this end an entire world of television programming has sprung up. The gospel needs to be carried into people's living rooms, we said. An empire of Christian entertainment has grown up, complete with films, drama groups, rock and folk music, and celebrities. Evangelicals eagerly welcome people like Bob Dylan or Paul Stookey into the Faith: now the Word will get out since here is someone who already commands an enormous hearing.

These enterprises all came under the headings "witnessing" and "missions" for us. I was brought up with a lively sense of duty to tell my friends and chance contacts, as well as the remote heathen, about Christ. "Ye shall be witnesses unto me," said Jesus to His disciples at the Ascension.[7] "Be ready always to give an answer to every man that asketh you a reason of the hope that is in you," said Saint Peter.[8] These texts spurred us to memorize Scripture so that it would be on the tips of our tongues if we found chances to witness. Whereas you might find a certain diffidence if you collared a Roman Catholic or a liberal Presbyterian on the street and shouted, "What must I do to be saved?" you would be fairly sure of getting an answer if your passer-by happened to be an evangelical.

Closely attached to this stress on witnessing, or "personal work" as we called it, was the matter of missions. Although foreign missionary work has a very ancient pedigree in the Church, we did not much speak of such men as Saint Martin of Tours, Saint Ninian, Saints Cyril and Methodius, or Saint Francis Xavier when we thought about missions. We tended to discover the wellsprings of world evangelization in the eighteenth and nineteeth centuries when men like Henry Martyn, William Carey, and Hudson Taylor set sail. Our emphasis on foreign missions, oddly, would have put us somewhat closer to the Catholics than to the Reformers since Luther, Calvin, and Zwingli, whom we held in the highest honor, are not remembered principally for having fostered this overseas travel in quite the same way as the Catholics and evangelicals have done.

Foreign missionary service was at the top of the hierarchy of callings for us. The order went something like this: jungle missionary work; then other foreign mission work in some city like Rangoon, Algiers, or Chungking; then preaching; then "Christian work," which meant joining the staff of a Christian periodical perhaps, or an evangelistic task-force like Youth For Christ; then secular work, the idea here being that God needed some people in the world to be witnesses right in the marketplace.

But there was no question, at least in my own imagination, that jungle missionary work was the noblest calling. The man with the pith helmet and Bible, slogging in knee-deep mud through the Congo, formed a sort of unofficial icon for me. We all had a picture, perhaps apocryphal, of David Livingstone dead on his knees in his hut, worn out with carrying the gospel to the ends of the earth. (David Livingstone, however, was never quite in the first rank of our undoubted heroes; there were too many ambiguities about his life, and about what, exactly, he preached. We liked his intrepidity, but we did not hear as much about him as we did about William Carey and Hudson Taylor.)

The Will of God

The corollary to all of this was that we had as our first priority the matter of finding the will of God for our lives. This meant quite literally that you began at an early age to ask God in your prayers to show you what He wanted you to do in life. The idea was that sooner or later, by means of circumstances, Scripture, and inner conviction, God would make clear to you whether you were to go to China with the China Inland Mission, or to Kenya with the Africa Inland Mission, or to Chicago with Youth For Christ. Perhaps—*perhaps*—He might want you on Wall Street, bearing witness at Morgan Guaranty. More probably He would have Vermont or Kentucky in mind, with Village Missions or Child Evangelism Fellowship, if your place was not to be overseas.

Implicit in this outlook on things was the assumption that the human race may be divided into the saved and the unsaved. Otherwise witnessing and foreign missionary work seemed somewhat ill-conceived. Here again we had Scripture and tradition on our side. The New Testament talks stridently and unabashedly about these two categories; and the Catholic church teaches that there is no salvation outside the Church.

It must be said in behalf of our charity, however, that any talk of one's playmates' being among the damned was virtually nonexistent. Naturally, if evangelical doctrine had been pressed home every time, some such conclusion would have been reached. But your imagination stopped a bit short of that. You were not thinking, "Bingy is going to hell," as you played with him in the sandbox (I had a friend named Bingy). You hoped, if you thought about it at all, that one day Bingy might hear the gospel and believe it. Things became awkward if you felt you yourself should attempt Bingy's conversion. Suddenly the whole gospel became wildly confusing, and you fumbled about among the phrases and eventually gave it up as a bad job.

This terrible experience was not confined to children. Many an unhappy evangelical has sat, writhing and perspiring, wondering how to open up a conversation and witness to the man sunk in his newspaper next to him on the plane. For sheer discomfort it is an experience not unlike being pressed to death. And it is almost indescribable to nonevangelical Christians who are not nearly so hagridden with the sense of responsibility on this front.

Behavior

If the human race may be divided into the saved and the unsaved, there is a further distinction that crops up among evangelical Christians. It arises over the matter of "separation."

The word refers to a number of points at which Christian behavior will differ from worldly behavior. It does not so much refer to outright sin (pillage, concupiscence, piracy) as to certain marginal but highly visible items. Often evangelicalism has been identified in the eyes of the world by means of these points. Wheaton College, for example, doubtless the best-known evangelical college in the world, will perhaps never surmount its reputation here, no matter what pure scholarship it produces.

Everyone knows that certain groups of Christians refrain from this or that activity for conscience' sake. The Amish drive buggies and hold their clothes together with hooks and eyes rather than with buttons; the Mennonites won't fight; Baptists are not supposed to drink alcohol; Catholics used to eschew flesh on Fridays. The list of items in the evangelicalism of my own childhood included smoking, drinking, dancing, cards (bridge, that is, not Old Maid), movies (*all* movies, until the borders broke down with Walt Disney, World War II news-reels, Cinerama, and finally television), gambling, theater, ballet, Sunday papers, mowing the lawn on Sunday, lipstick, and certain baubles which included earrings, but not rings, necklaces, or bracelets.

The matter of religious conscience is a matter of the greatest delicacy. It touches on some of the noblest instincts of man-kind. One does not jeer at a Hindu woman for wearing a dot of red on her face, nor at a Moslem for touching his forehead to the ground, nor at a Quaker for refusing to vote, nor at a Jew for wrapping himself in a shawl and bawling his prayers at the corner of 111th Street and Broadway. All of these customs en-tail taboo.

All tribes, cultures, and religions have known that taboo lies deep in the human grain. The absence of taboo means that hu-man life has sunk to a bestial level. There is a reason for every item on anybody's list of taboos, and outsiders have to ap-proach the topic gingerly.

What might be written as a superscript over the entire evan-gelical list of taboos is the word *cleanliness*. Saint Paul teaches, for example, that the human body is the temple of the Holy Ghost; hence, evangelicals have objected to poisons like nicotine being absorbed into this shrine. Long before the sur-geon general started waving everyone away from tobacco, we were in there waving. As for alcohol, we would have pointed out that whatever may be said for it as a social lubricant, it is a dangerous substance contributing little to good health. We felt that bonhomie ought to arise from true fellowship, not from the haze of inebriation.

As for dancing, it sails too near the wind: here is one body, so full of the heat of desire, pressed to another, only fanning flames that ought rather to be dampened. This heat should be saved for the holy sacrament of marriage.

Cards: evangelicals had an idea—and who knows what truth is in it—that the origin of playing cards is all shot through with cabalistic and even obscene hints and that therefore it is just as

13

well to stay clear of the whole business.

Movies: Hollywood is an evil place, and Christians should not support an industry that emanates from a purlieu like that. Besides, what you see in most movies is very far from encouraging virtue. The same goes for theater.

Ballet: the tutus and tights are much too brief and revealing. Somehow modesty is being violated.

Gambling: it is a manifest evil and at best a waste of time and a misuse of money.

Sunday: it is the Lord's Day, and every possible routine activity should be set aside, not because God wants the day to be dull but because the principle of a sabbath rest is woven into the fabric of Creation itself.

Lipstick and baubles: paints and bangles have always been the marks of heathendom. Christian womanhood should be adorned with modesty and charity. The world ought to be able to perceive a beauty that does not owe itself to the cosmetic industry, which is, after all, a form of fraud since its appeal is to vanity, promising as it does to make us look younger and more beautiful than we really are.

Thus would run the rationale offered by the evangelicalism of my own background on these points. We thought of the early Christians, who absented themselves from Rome's amusements and manners.

No single mode of life can settle the matter, of course. There will always be a paradox in Christian behavior, with Jesus dining and winebibbing on one hand, and Saint John the Baptist living a fiercely ascetic life on the other. Benedictine sparseness or rococo plenitude? Quaker quietude or Pentecostal noise? Total abstinence or gratitude for wine? The Christian gospel itself is fraught with paradoxes and mysteries, and no one style will exhaust its amplitude.

Conscience and Piety

All of this bespeaks what, in my opinion, is the supreme

hallmark of evangelicalism, namely, its extremely tender conscience. Evangelicals are not at all cavalier or swashbuckling about matters of piety and spirituality, much less about morals. If the Bible says no cursing, then the discussion is over. It is a sin to toy with God's Word or make light of biblical injunctions. Evangelicals can never be saucy about sexual matters. They cannot pretend to be blameless, but the note struck in their preaching and teaching is that there is only one legitimate context for sexual activity; monogamous, heterosexual marriage. Even to record this is to invite catcalls nowadays, and hardly an evangelical family remains unscathed on this front. Nevertheless, evangelicalism itself makes no attempt to update biblical morality in the interest of winning greater autonomy and variety for us all. It is piquant that the evangelicals' most powerful ally and advocate in these matters is someone whom many of them in the past looked on as the Antichrist, namely, the Bishop of Rome.

Evangelical spirituality stands or falls with private Bible reading. This answers to its doctrinal stress on the Bible alone as the touchstone. In some sense evangelicalism is very Judaic on this point; almost the whole duty of the Jews was to fill their children's minds with the Law of the Lord.

In the household where I grew up, family prayers occurred twice a day. At 7:30 in the morning we all went from breakfast into the living room. With my mother playing the piano we sang a hymn, after which my father read the Bible to us. Then we knelt down, facing into the overstuffed chairs with our elbows sunk in the cushions, and my father led us in prayer, all of us joining in the Lord's Prayer at the end. There was no awkwardness surrounding the rite. It was as natural as washing the dishes. In the evening we stayed at the dinner table, and again my father read and prayed.

Sunday school took us to the Bible as well. Its agenda concentrated almost exclusively on familiarizing us with the text of Scripture. Bible stories were told and retold, often illustrated with a device called flannelgraph, in which the teacher stood by an easel and put up small paper figures on the flannel-covered board as she told, say, of Abraham's servant's going out to find a bride for Isaac.

To this day biblical events remain in my imagination as they appeared on the flannelgraph. There were little palm trees and stone altars and even a rock for Jacob's pillow. There was also a wonderful celestial ladder, shot through with light, on which the angels descended and ascended in Jacob's dream. A rain of burning sulphur rocks falling out of the sky onto the little walled city of Sodom (you could get a whole city quite handily in one cutout) will aways be the picture for me, no matter what we are told by scholars about what never happened back there.

Evangelical Sunday schools are not full of demurrals about "myth" and "legend." Tell the story as though it were God's own story, says evangelicalism. Nothing is gained by endless hemming and hawing. Faith cannot feed on that.

Evangelical spirituality centers, finally, on personal daily devotions, also called "quiet time." Just as all Christian traditions enjoin some sort of regular private exercises for the faithful (the Rosary, the Order for Morning Prayer, or some other aid), so the evangelicals emphasize the reading of the Bible itself. They find something farcical in the religious profession of people who voice loud opinions on God, prayer, or the spiritual life but who never pray or read the Bible. Seminarians who march in the streets and offer opinions on social matters but who say that Bible reading and private prayer have long since disappeared for them do not attract the evangelical imagination. Even more odd is the theologian who says briskly that he may find Jesus in the local bar or massage parlor but certainly not in cold and musty *churches*. One wonders just who it is, then, that people find in these musty churches.

The actual frame of mind of an evangelical as he comes to the Bible in his daily devotions is a matter of some importance. His whole ambition is to "get a blessing." This can take on a somewhat magical aspect at times. I can remember struggling

16

to wring spiritual counsel from the lists of names in 1 Chronicles or from the hair-raising tales of butchery in Judges. Generally speaking, however, the attempt turns out to yield fruit if it is pursued consistently. There is an agile immediacy about an evangelical's attitude towards Scripture.

Evangelical prayer is extempore. We learned at a very early age to pray aloud with great aplomb. Usually we embarked on prayers with "Our dear heavenly Father, we just want to praise and thank Thee...." This was a safe start. We distrusted such openings as "Almighty God," or "Eternal God," since liberal Protestants tended to approach Him that way, and we thought that they had perhaps not really met Him intimately.

The acid test of vocal prayer came at the end of the prayer, however. If someone finished his petition or thanksgiving with a bald "Amen," he gave everything away. He was not one of us. A true evangelical used the scriptural formula, asking it all in the name of Our Lord Jesus Christ, or, in the shorter phrase, "...in Jesus' name, Amen."

If Bible reading and prayer form the taproot of evangelical spirituality, then fellowship is the characteristic activity. All Christians will agree that fellowship in Christ is the bond that actually unites them to other Christians, rather than race, family, money, class, or taste.

But evangelicals have made a major specialty out of fellowship. They *talk* to each other about the Lord. They meet in groups whose sole purpose is to bring Christians together for informal Bible study, often without any teacher, and for prayer and "sharing." They speak openly about their inner burdens and about what God is teaching them. They find the embarrassed and tongue-tied religion of other Christian traditions incomprehensible. "Let the redeemed of the Lord say so!" was an extremely popular biblical text in my own church.

Testimonies play a major role in evangelical spirituality. In a testimony someone stands and says something about his present experience of the Lord. He might recount some vic-

17

tory in his personal life, such as the overcoming of some temptation, or perhaps tell of a decision that God has helped him make.

No account of the atmosphere in evangelicalism would be complete without some reference to its hymnody. It is difficult for nonevangelical Christians to appreciate the place occupied by hymn-singing among evangelicals. We sang and sang. Isaac Watts, William Cowper, John Newton, Charles Wesley—these were the big names. My father would sit down at the piano as he came through the living room at odd moments and play "When All Thy Mercies, O My God," or "There Is a Fountain Filled with Blood," or "Praise Him, Praise Him, Jesus Our Blessed Redeemer."

Evangelicals draw mainly on eighteenth- and nineteenth-century hymnody for their "worship" hymns, but nineteenth- and twentieth-century revivalist hymns and gospel songs form a major part of the literature. "Jesus Saves," "Blessed Assurance," and "When the Roll Is Called Up Yonder" are favorites, as are "Since Jesus Came into My Heart" and "There's Power in the Blood." There is also an enormous number of "choruses," such as "Every Day with Jesus," and "Safe Am I."

During the latter 1940s the Inter-Varsity Christian Fellowship performed a great service for our wing of evangelicalism by publishing a hymnal for student use that included a number of hymns hitherto unknown to most of us. Charles Wesley's "And Can It Be That I Should Gain" and Horatius Bonar's "I Hear the Words of Love" and others like these vastly enriched devotion for us. Groups of us met to do nothing but sing these hymns, hour after hour. They seemed to give shape to our experience of God and to articulate sentiments that would otherwise have remained somewhat amorphous. Later, when I came upon written prayers and the liturgy, I recalled this sense in which pre-set forms of words such as we have in hymns, far from quelling devotion or cramping the liberty of the Spirit, actually seemed to nourish devotion and give an infinitely larger notion of liberty than we would otherwise have had.

Why, Then, the Journey?

The obvious question that arises in the light of what I have sketched here is, Why set out on a pilgrimage at all? If home base was that good, what is there to seek? If the Reformation may be credited with fostering this sort of Christian earnestness, zeal, and fidelity, where else would anyone want to turn?

2

Spirit and Flesh:
Sundered Forever or Reunited?

One day when I was about twelve a friend of mine and I were out on our bicycles. We found ourselves going past his church, and he asked me if I would like to look in. The idea sent a small thrill through me, as though he had suggested that we buy some cigarettes or a pin-up calendar (there was no pornography in those days, at least none that you could buy over the counter).

I had been past this church innumerable times, but I had never been inside. The tall thin spire and the gray stone of the arches seemed to bespeak centuries of august tradition that lay quite outside the orbit of my own world.

An Introduction to Symbolism

When we got inside, the first thing that struck me was how dark it was. Religious light from the stained glass lay dimly on things, creating a kind of holy dusk. I felt I was in the precincts of great mysteries. We stood whispering in the aisle.

My friend had bowed in the direction of the altar as we came in. Clearly he was familiar with a protocol that was unknown to me. This presented an indefinable situation, since it was I, not he, who was the literate Christian believer, I thought: he was a mere churchgoer. It was I who knew the Scriptures and, hence, knew what altars really meant. It was I who knew the gospel and, hence, what pulpits were for. I was the one who could cite the texts about the Light of the World, which these candlesticks only suggested. And yet my world was devoid of any of this furniture, whereas, obviously he knew what to do amongst it all. I was embarrassed over having to appear ignorant on any point and tried to seem knowledgeable. It would have been inappropriate for me to be cast in the role of inquirer: this would have thrown a false light on things since, if there were to be any question of my ever witnessing to him, I would have had to maintain a slight edge when it came to knowing about these things.

My most vivid recollection from that visit was of a tiny prick of light from a lamp hanging near the altar. I did not know what it might be, but it lodged itself forever in the firmament of my memory, like Arcturus or some other infinitely remote star. I was filled with awe, and even something like rapture, at how beautiful, how august, everything was.

How was I to account for the impression that all of this made on me? I would have been able to argue my friend down, I think, if either of us had broached the topic of how his church differed from mine. But neither of us did. I had been too impressed.

That, perhaps, is not without significance. A twelve-year-old boy is impressionable. But what had I been impressed with?

Beauty, of course. But beyond that, what I had seen was an array of symbols. It seemed that all the things that I had read about in the holy Scriptures concerning the majesty of God, the centrality of the Lord Jesus Christ, the mysteries of Creation and Redemption were suddenly on display here. Nothing in this backdrop was actually strange to me. I knew the Scripture from one end to the other and could have told my friend about the whole lineage of altars from Abel to the Apocalypse. This furniture recalled the huge drama of Redemption, which I knew and believed in the greatest possible detail. I could also have quoted texts from Hebrews to the effect that earthly altars were done away with at the cross. Did all these symbols—altar, candles, cross, and perhaps even the sumptuous windows—lean too far towards idolatry? Certainly they had the effect of complicating and elaborating things. Could "the simplicity that is in Christ"[9] somehow be lost in an array such as this?

My own church had an open Bible with gilded edges painted onto the plaster wall behind the pulpit. We were given pictures in Sunday school to color and take home. There was a small silver cross ornamenting the lid of the tray in which the thimble-like Communion glasses were arranged. I was, therefore, not a stranger to Christian symbolism. The men took off their hats in my church also: surely that was a symbolic act? And the pulpit stood at the center of focus in the front. I knew that this was more than an acoustic arrangement; it symbolized the centrality of the preached Word. At Christmas a manger scene was set up at the front of the church.

Obviously, then, we could never have argued, like Islam, that all recognizable symbols are inadmissible. My friend's church had many symbols; we had some. Where the line might be drawn I did not know. When, years later, I worshiped with a group of Christians who strove for a nonsymbolic simplicity even greater than that sought by my childhood church, I noticed that here the table was placed in the center, with pews arranged around it, signifying the centrality of the Lord's Supper for this group. It is difficult to eliminate symbolism.

Christian imagination differs over details, but all Christian imagination attaches importance to symbols. Whether it is a matter of lowering one's voice in the building where the church meets, or of refusing to use make-up, or of wearing or not wearing a crucifix, or of kneeling, or bowing one's head to say grace or bowing at the holy name, or folding one's hands or crossing oneself, all Christian piety and worship is shot through with the symbolism of either gesture or objects or both. We see the unseen in the seen. The surface of things bespeaks what lies beneath. Our postures, our dress, our gestures, and the artifacts with which we surround ourselves—the very way we bind and gild our Bibles—all cry out that we are creatures whose approach to the Most High, since it cannot be direct like the seraphim's, must be set about and assisted with symbols.

None of us is a bare intellect. Our eyes see colors; our noses smell fragrances; our fingers feel textures.

The common stuff of our mortal life is girded with symbols: wedding rings, diplomas, medals, badges, handshakes, flags, uniforms, birthday candles, Christmas wrappings, bridal gowns, school colors, roses, lilies, kisses, even table settings. All of these gestures, clothes, and artifacts say something. They convey meaning to us. If we reflect for a moment, we will find that words are very far from being the only bearers of meaning to us mortals. Everything we see, hear, taste, smell, and touch cries out to us. Fiery red, dusty rose, indigo, periwinkle, salmon, avocado, toast, mushroom—we go to great trouble to choose colors for our walls, fabrics, and clothes. These things matter. They create an ambience. They determine the environment in which our ordinary lives move.

The very wish to escape this principle testifies to it. The spareness of Puritan and Quaker decor and the subdued blues and grays and blacks of homespun cloth bespeak simplicity, sobriety, and dignity. The smell of tarragon, gardenia, leaf smoke, seaweed, or cologne smite us and rouse us. The smells of carbon monoxide, offal, decay, and bile also smite us and rouse us. We are obliged to respond. Textures—velvet, tweed, horses' noses, silky hair, creamy skin, stubbly chins, bread dough—we are creatures whose lives are set amongst textures.

Some religions beckon us away from all of this. Some even abominate it all. It is illusion, they tell us. It is all sordid and doomed and worthless. These religions drive a wedge between us mortals and all that we know of life. They tell us to be spiritual, by which they mean that we must strive to become disembodied; ghosts; souls.

Historic Christianity, on the other hand, cries *"Benedicite!"* It calls out "Glory be to God for dappled things!" It lauds and extols the One who is the fountainhead of all shapes, colors, textures, sounds, and smells. The Most High did not create a charade or a trap when He made all of this. The Creation rushes from His superabundant freedom and love and cries out in exultation to Him. No least thing is silent. The timid and beady eye of a fieldmouse, the fife of the winter wren, the bubbling of water falling over rocks or boiling in a kettle, roars of laughter from a room full of friends, the murmur of a loved one's voice: what does it all say but "Hosanna!"

Ah, but those things are of the earth earthy, says the spiritual man. We must set our affections on things above, not on things on the earth. Here we have no continuing city. The world passeth away and the lust thereof. This will all be folded up as a garment. Since this is so, we must tailor our worship and piety accordingly. Textures and colors and smells have no place here. The locale of true spirituality is in the heart. It is enough that we hear the words of salvation and meditate on them in our hearts.

What Is Symbolic?

My own church encouraged a nonsymbolistic line of thought. We distrusted the symbolism of colors and shapes and gestures, *at least when they were attached to worship*, since this seemed to bring things very near to idolatry. We invoked the commandment forbidding graven images.

If, however, that commandment did indeed mean, flatly, that we mortals must not make anything with our hands that looks like anything in Creation, then we would have had to go through our own houses and throw out all the stuffed animals from the children's beds, and all the pictures from the walls, and all of the Hummel figures and wood carvings from the bric-a-brac shelves. We would never have paid homage at the Lincoln or Jefferson Memorials, since these shrines were dominated by huge graven images. We would have had to adopt the rigorous Islamic approach to the matter.

It may be that there are Christian groups who attempt this.

We ourselves made no pretense of anything so austere, however. If someone had asked us about the commandment forbidding graven images, and we had suddenly remembered all the stuffed and graven images in our own houses, and the Lincoln Memorial, we would perhaps have urged that it is *religious* statuary that is forbidden. In urging this, we would perhaps have come a step towards what the commandment actually seems to forbid, namely, the *worshiping* of anything man-made. That is how it is phrased; you are not to make images representing anything in heaven, earth, or hell, and proceed to worship them. Clearly, the divine Law does not place a blanket prohibition on the making of graven things, or even graven things for religious use. The very God who promulgated the Law then went on to order golden cherubim for His Ark and enormous cast bulls to hold the brazen sea in His Temple.

But our view of what churches should look like did not stand or fall with the commandment. Even if we could have been satisfied that what is forbidden is strictly idol worship and not the whole world of whittling and casting and sculpting, we would have pressed home the idea that Christian worship has its locale in the heart. It concerns itself with the unseen. We do not need the vast height of ribbed vaulting and the dim religious light of colored glass and the smoke of incense to rouse our spirits to worship God. Indeed, those things address the earthy man. We are told that we must worship God in spirit and in truth.

Yes, says Christianity. A clapboard chapel, a Harlem storefront, or a kitchen table may form the setting for true Christian worship, just as truly as the cathedral at Chartres may. God does not dwell in houses made with hands in any event. But to point this out is not quite to have established the clapboard chapel, the storefront, or the kitchen table as better or worse than the cathedral. It is merely to have pointed out something crucial to the gospel, namely, that no matters of taste, wealth, geography, pedigree, or intelligence are laid down as prerequisites for any man's approach to God. If someone is a child, an ignoramus, or a dunce, he may offer his adoration to the Most High just as acceptably as kings and philosophers may. Indeed, there is some reason to suppose that the child and the fool may have an easier time of it here, if we catch the drift of what Christ says.

There are matters of much greater moment at stake than merely how to build and furnish the church. All Christian groups, including Brethren, Quakers, and Mennonites, attach some dignity to the church building, and in so doing they evince from afar the same principle that is at work in Chartres. Insofar as we go to any pains at all to make the structure pleasing and to make its shape and atmosphere answer to the solemnity of what goes on inside we testify to the principle that the surface of things matters. Forms and colors matter. If we want simplicity, dignity, and quiet, then let us make the building answer to these unseen qualities in the very bricks, wood, and paint that we choose. If we want to cry out, *"Ad maiorem Dei gloriam!"* then let us make the building answer to this acclamation in the very stones, wood, and colors that we choose. No one will want to evoke the atmosphere of the vaudeville or the tavern in his place of worship. If his group comes into possession of an old welding shop or strip joint, there will surely be some redecorating.

The Heart of the Matter

We must press the matter further. Since Christian worship is a spiritual matter, should we not make every effort to minimize the external accoutrements so that no one will be fooled by mere "atmosphere" into supposing that his elevated feelings are worship when they are nothing but aesthetic impressionability?

The question touches on something crucial. Exalted feelings by no means guarantee that real worship is going on in the heart. Chances to fool oneself lie all about. The minute we see this, we also realize that these chances are as lively in a simple meeting hall or at a kitchen table as they are at Chartres. Familiar phrases in public prayers, familiar and consoling texts from Scripture, favorite tunes, and humble and good people are very good things, and who will not thank God for them or pretend that they do not warm his soul? They are good, but the euphoria that is experienced here is not quite synonymous with worship, any more than is the euphoria experienced by the aesthete who is transported by the strains of *"O Esca Viatorum"* sung by the boy choristers in the lofty dimness of King's College Chapel in Cambridge.

We all know what powerful and good feelings may be aroused when Christians meet together. A throng of apple-cheeked Germans singing *"Ein Feste Burg ist Unser Gott,"* or a throng of Welshmen singing *"Cwm Rhondda,"* or a throng of Baptists singing "Jesus Saves!" with trumpet trio and Hammond organ at the Sunday night service—these are thrilling occasions. We reach the last note and feel we may ascend into heaven itself. Smaller and quieter scenes may also affect us deeply: a group holding hands in a circle at a campfire, heads bowed, sharing simple and earnest prayers; two of us riding in a car, talking, like the two on the way to Emmaus, until our hearts burn within us because God is there; or a communion service where somehow all the hymns and prayers and homilies have worked together to form a flawless whole.

If worship is to be rigorously detached from all sentiment, and even from sentimentalism, then we will all have to conclude that it is inaccessible. Who of us can achieve a pristine state of spirit beyond the reach of "lesser" elements like good feelings, familiarity, solidarity, beauty, and warmth? Perhaps the seraphim can behold the white light of the Divine Glory directly. Ancient tradition says so. But we are not seraphim. That glory comes to us mortals through a dome of many-colored glass, which must include our emotions as well as virtues like charity and purity of heart.

The Word Became Flesh

At the root of these questions, which first presented themselves to me as my friend and I stood whispering in the nave of that dim church, lies the Incarnation itself. For in that event, heaven came down to us. The Eternal Word became flesh. God became man. The spiritual became physical.

To say this is to repeat the obvious. All Christians agree on this. But not all Christian teaching encourages us to look into the matter. What might it mean?

Whatever else the great mystery of the Incarnation may mean, surely it suggests that the terrible and tragic rip in the fabric of Creation is being reknit. To see this, we must recall Eden.

In Eden the web of Creation was seamless. Man was in perfect harmony with his environment, placed there as a vassal to rule it and as a priest to bless God for it. There was no disjuncture anywhere—between man and woman, or between them and other living creatures either animal or angelic, or between man and himself. It is even possible to suppose that no such thing as "self-consciousness" existed, since to be conscious of oneself is already to have placed some distance between a man and his own identity, with a scrutinizing self set over against a self that simply lives life. Innocency would seem to imply some such state of affairs originally, and our loss of this pellucid and unflawed simplicity is part of our tragedy.

This vision of seamlessness would also oblige us to suppose that no disjuncture lay between one part of creation and another—between the physical world and the nonphysical, for example. All things existed in harmony, not in a blur or a confusion, but a continuum, like a musical scale or the spectrum of colors. Diamonds, soil, clams, eagles, men, angels, seraphim: here was the created order. Over against this stood only one other order, the Uncreated. The distance lay not between the "physical" and the "spiritual" so much as between the created and the Uncreated.

In the harmony of Eden, everything that we did constituted an unceasing oblation of praise to the Most High. We needed no liturgy there—no setting aside of a special hour when we might turn away from the jumble of our activities and compose ourselves and offer to God the sacrifice of praise. There was *nothing but* liturgy. "The work of the people," which is what the word *liturgy* means, included our eating and drinking and resting and loving as well as our work, which we experienced not as drudgery but as freedom since we were perfectly suited to it and perfectly empowered to carry it out. Like the angels who praise God continuously no matter what errands they are on, we lived in the fullness of ceaseless adoration to God. Our activity was our oblation. Simply being human—having been made in the image of God—constituted our dignity, and we bore this dignity before seraphim and archangels as a unique testimony to God's glory.

This was all torn apart at the Fall. We wrecked Creation by making a grab and saying, "This much of it shall be our own." The fabric ripped. Now, instead of the sacred seamlessness in which every fiber of Creation was knit together in a pattern that blazoned the glory of God, we had a torn garment. The poor remnant we clutched in our fists was *secular*, in the most tragic sense of the word: that which is not acknowledged as God's. It is a noncategory, of course, since nothing that exists belongs to anyone but God.

But evil is always illusion. It insists on the lie that we can have something for ourselves. This is the sole principle at work in hell. Lucifer chose to believe it; or, since it is unimaginable that he actually could have believed it, then we may say that he chose to pretend it might be. Very well, says Truth, you may pretend this. But the pretense will be, literally, your undoing. It will unmake you. You will have opted for something that is not, namely, a lie. Hell is built of lies.

In this sense we may be said to have introduced hell into our world at the Fall. For here we introduced the lie that we may have something of our own. Whatever the fruit that we snatched at may have been, it was not for us. We decided, however, that it should be ours nonetheless. This was a lie, and the result was division. The secular divided from the sacred: it is a complete falsehood, but we must live with it for the rest of our sad history.

The idea that there was a "secular" order of activity that would occupy us for most of our waking and sleeping hours, distinct from some fugitive "sacred" moments when we pray or worship, never came from God. It is a lie, and the disjunctures in life now testify to this.

Our work, formerly synonymous with our freedom and dignity, is now drudgery. It breaks our backs. Childbearing, presumably in some sense the crown of human experience—something that we, made in the image of God, would experience and that angels only could envy—is now marred with pain. Our bodies, the very statuary of God so to speak, are now torn from our spirits in the ultimate division called death, which yields in the place of the noble creature called man two pitiable horrors, a corpse and a ghost. When the physical is divided from the spiritual, there results the cacophony that brays and clashes in the abyss outside the harmony of the divine order. Division. Hell.

The Incarnation reverses all of this. Our salvation from that abyss and division comes to us in the figure of God–made–man. Spirit and flesh are knit once more into perfect integrity. The heresies have tried to make the Incarnation an illusion— God's merely "coming upon" the man, or tenanting there briefly. False religions perpetuate the great divide between flesh and spirit, rather than between good and evil where Christianity says it lies.

The Flesh and the Spirit

Even Christian piety itself has had a difficult time fending off the error. Using Saint Paul's language about flesh and spirit, this piety has often spoken as though to be holy ("spiritual") is to be more or less disembodied. Since that is obviously not possible, we will do our best to keep spiritual things distinct from physical things. There will be "the spiritual life" and "the ordinary life." There will be sacred activities and secular activities. When we are praying, we are closer to the center of things than when we are washing dishes, changing diapers, driving in a traffic jam, or sitting in a committee meeting: thus would run this piety.

This is to misread Saint Paul. He never meant his word *spiritual* to mean disembodied. To be spiritual for Saint Paul was to have brought everything back to God where it belongs and where it was in Eden. It is to have had one's life knit back together so that it is no longer secular and divided, but whole. It is to have become one with Christ in whom dwells all the fullness of God bodily. Christ is the great icon and paradigm of this wholeness. In Him we see the fullness of God in bodily form, and we are called to that wholeness, not to disembodied angelic life. The Christian religion, far from driving a wedge between them, knits the spiritual and the physical back together.

"The flesh," as Saint Paul used the term, refers, ironically, not to our bodies but to fallen human nature. The "carnal" spirit is the one that devours things for itself and refuses to make them an oblation to God. The carnal spirit is cruel, egocentric, avaricious, gluttonous, and lecherous, and as such is fevered, restless, and divided. The spiritual man, on the other hand, is alone the man who both knows what flesh is for and can enter into its amplitude. The lecher, for example, supposes that he knows more about love than the virgin or the continent man. He knows nothing. Only the virgin and the faithful spouse know what love is about. The glutton supposes that he knows the pleasures of food, but the true knowledge of food is unavailable to his dribbling and surfeited jowls. The difference between the carnal man and the spiritual man is not physical. They may look alike and weigh the same. The difference lies, rather, between one's being divided, snatching and grabbing at things, even nonphysical things like fame and power, or being whole and receiving all things as Adam was meant to receive them, in order to offer them as an oblation to their Giver.

Insofar as Christian piety strives to detach itself from physical life and all the forms and colors of life, it goes astray. It is the *demand* for things that Christ sets us free from, not things themselves. It is slavery and striving that cease when He comes with His freedom. The spiritual man will not diminish his proper intake of food in order to make himself more spiritual, except for the specific and temporary purpose of fasting. It is gluttony that he will avoid, realizing that gluttony is bondage. The spiritual man will not love the music of Mozart or the taste of wine less because he is a Christian, but music and wine will not exist for him as things he demands. In his freedom he will have learned to receive them as they are given and to make them an oblation of thanksgiving.

The Incarnation, then transfigures the whole fabric of life for us and delivers it back to us and us back to it in the seamlessness that we lost at our exile from Eden. Once again we may stand in our proper relation to things, as lords over them and not as their slaves. Once more we stand in our true Adam-like dignity because of the Second Adam and may begin to learn anew the solemn office for which we were created, namely, to bless God and to lead the whole Creation in that blessing. Our flesh, having been worn by the Most High Himself, is the most noble mantle of all. The Manichaeans and Buddhists and Platonists on the one hand, who belittle this flesh, and the gluttons and lechers and egoists on the other, who are slaves to it, are still living in division. Only in the Incarnation may we find the knitting back together of the fabric into its true integrity.

If our religion draws us away from the plain fabric of life, and if it encourages in us the notion that Monday through Saturday are mostly secular, and if it crimps our freedom to join hilariously in all that is good in life, then, be we Bible-believing to the core, something is askew. If piety suggests to a musician that to play his violin or his trumpet in a church service is somehow more Christian than to play it in Carnegie Hall, then it is heresy. If it makes him timorous about being a creature of flesh and blood and pinches him into hesitancy about everything, then it has done him a disservice. If by its practice it implies that colors and symbols and gestures and ceremonies and smells are inappropriate for the house of the Lord and must be kept outside, for "secular" and domestic celebrations like birthdays, parades, weddings, and Christmas banquets, then it has driven a wedge between his deepest human yearnings and the God who made them.

Evangelicalism: Correct but Incomplete?

The evangelicalism of my childhood church taught me true doctrine about the Incarnation. It taught me about Creation and about Eden and about the Fall. But somehow it never, at least in its piety, put Humpty-Dumpty back together again. For evangelicals, there seemed to be "the world," which meant almost everything that makes up human life, and there was "the spiritual life." One tried to steer the right course. The responsibilities and routines that make up most of life, as well as the music and the colors that gild life, were legitimate certainly, but somehow we were left with tensions and uncertainties. Should one go into "Christian" work or secular work? It was a false question and presented an even more false answer, since it permitted us to look for an answer by weighing religious organizations against secular ones, supposing that the one offered Christian work to us while the other offered only secular work. A whole array of pickets had been thrown up between us and civilization's lovely diversions such as ballet, theater, cinema, and wine, and each point had its rationale, certainly. But the net effect was to plant in our imaginations the notion that spirituality was more a matter of excision than of transfiguration.

Undoubtedly the place where evangelical vision may most

readily be observed at a glance is in its church buildings.

As I stood with my friend in his church that day, I was on familiar gound insofar as I recognized what the various appointments alluded to: the cross, the altar, the candles, and so forth. But I was on very strange ground insofar as these things were actually represented here in the visible world of my bodily experience. "Christian truth" should be kept *un*bodied, I believed. It was for my heart, not my eyes.

There is one sense in which this is true, and the Reformation has a lively sense of how prone we all are to magic and idolatry. We mortals would much rather bob at the cross than embrace its truth in our hearts. To light candles is much easier for us than to be consumed with the self-giving fire of charity so effectively symbolized by those candles. We lavish respect on the altar at the front of the church and neglect the sacrifice of a pure heart. Evangelicalism presses home these observations, quite rightly.

But it is one thing to see dangers; it is another to be true to the Faith in all of its amplitude. By avoiding the dangers of magic and idolatry on the one hand, evangelicalism runs itself very near the shoals of Manichaeanism on the other—the view, that is, that pits the spiritual against the physical. Its bare, spare churches, devoid of most Christian symbolism (except, oddly, *some* candles, or perhaps a modest cross in some of its churches), bespeak its correct attempt to keep the locale of faith where it must ultimately be, in the heart of man. But by denying to the whole realm of Christian life and practice the principle that it allows in all the other realms of life, namely, the principle of symbolism and ceremony and imagery, it has, despite its loyalty to orthodox doctrine, managed to give a semi-Manichaean *hue* to the Faith.

If someone had asked me why we disallowed crosses on the one hand but at the same time permitted wedding rings, which are, after all, solid objects in the physical world whose sole function is to represent and embody something that exists in a much more profound realm, I am not sure what answer I would have given. I had heard it said, especially with respect to the crucifix, that we worshiped a risen Christ, not a dead one. This eventually came to sound facile to me, since no Christian can pretend that the Cross does not stand forever as focal for Christian vision; to pit the Resurrection against it is flippant. Furthermore, the same people who said this had little objection to manger scenes; they would have jibbed, however, if someone had asked them if they worshiped a Christ who was still an infant.

The discussion ought not to become a quarrel. The eye that sees the dangers of idolatry is a true one. But to correct a flood, one does not want a drought. Because human beings are idolators one does not attempt to protect the gospel with four bare walls. It is false to pit the visible world of solid objects against faith. We never do this in other realms of our experience. Indeed, we cannot, since we are physical creatures and not angels.

Reuniting the Physical and Spiritual

It is in the physical world that the intangible meets us. A kiss seals a courtship. The sexual act seals a marriage. A ring betokens the marriage. A diploma crowns years of schooling. A doctoral robe bespeaks intellectual achievement. A uniform and stripes announce a recruit's training. A crown girds the brow that rules England. This symbolism bespeaks the sort of creature we are. To excise all of this from piety and worship is to suggest that the gospel beckons us away from our humanity into a disembodied realm. It is to turn the Incarnation into a mere doctrine.

The Incarnation took all that properly belongs to our humanity and delivered it back to us, redeemed. All of our inclinations and appetites and capacities and yearnings and proclivities are purified and gathered up and glorified by Christ. He did not come to thin out human life; He came to set it free. All the dancing and feasting and processing and singing and building and sculpting and baking and merrymaking that belong to us, and that were stolen away into the service of false gods, are returned to us in the gospel.

The worship of God, surely, should be the place where men, angels, and devils may see human flesh once more set free into all that it was created to be. To restrict that worship to sitting in pews and listening to words spoken is to narrow things down in a manner strange to the gospel. We are creatures who are made to bow, not just spiritually (angels can do that) but with kneebones and neck muscles. We are creatures who cry out to surge in great procession, "*ad altare Dei,*" not just in our hearts (disembodied spirits can do that) but with our feet, singing great hymns with our tongues, our nostrils full of the smoke of incense.

Is it objected that this is too physical, too low down on the scale for the gospel? Noses indeed! If the objection carries the day, then we must jettison the stable and the manger, and the winepots at Cana, and the tired feet anointed with nard, and the splinters of the cross, not to say the womb of the mother who bore God when He came to us. Too physical? What do we celebrate in our worship? It is Buddhism and Platonism and Manichaeanism that tell us to disavow our flesh and expunge everything but thoughts. The gospel brings back all of our faculties with a rush.

It was evangelicalism that taught me to love Christ and to defend the doctrine of the Incarnation. It was also evangelicalism that taught me that the locale of true religion is in a man's heart and not on this mountain or that. Insofar as the simple forms of its worship stood out in protest against mere sumptuousness it was truly Protestant.

But is protest enough? Can the heart of man feed on protest? Is it enough for our piety to say that because an idolator bows we will refuse to do so? On this accounting, prayer itself would have to go, since idolators pray. It is like saying that since gluttons eat too much food, we will eat none. What is needed is someone who will show what the right use of food looks like.

Is it enough to keep pressing home the truth that God dwells not in temples made with hands and that therefore the church building is nothing? Where is the doctrine, then, of the Incarnation and of Redemption? It was not simply our souls that were rescued from hell: the whole Creation was redeemed, including space and time. Evangelicalism believes this and teaches it, as Saint Paul did in Romans 8, and as Saint John did in Revelation. If it is true, then may not the church building itself stand in our history and in our experience as itself a pledge and token, like a wedding ring, of this Redemption? In Christ, all of life is returned to its proper center. All human work is hallowed once more. But most people do not see this. Gas stations and hotels and restaurants and office buildings are not dedicated to God. But Christianity says that they should be. All work should be offered to God. Let us hallow at least this one place as a "sacred space," as we hallow the hour of worship as "sacred time."

Only symbols, of course. But who will think lightly of his wedding ring and say it is nothing? Who will take a kiss lightly? It is "only" a physical pledge of something deeper, more mysterious, and more substantial, namely, love. But in that small physical act the great mystery is somehow bespoken. Of course, God does not live in the church building, if by that we mean that He needs it for shelter and for a place to lay His head. He lives in heaven, we say. He makes His dwelling in the paths of the sea. He has also told us that His dwelling is in the heart of man. No one can teach otherwise.

These things, which are true, must somehow be focused and brought to a point in a symbol for us mortals. In prayer we focus and bring to a point the petitions and praises that are always going up from our innermost beings. In the singing of hymns we articulate what is formless and semiconscious the rest of the time. In the hour of worship we focus and bring to a point what should be true always of our hearts, namely, that God is adored there. Likewise, with the church building we set aside space and enclose it with walls and a roof, which shall be for us the token of what should be true of all spaces. Like the lamb that the ancient Jew brought from his flock, this space stands for all space as that lamb stood for the whole flock. The principle of focusing and bringing to a point did not disappear with the New Covenant. We mortals are still the same sort of creature. We cannot live with abstractions. We cannot nourish ourselves on generalities. The Incarnation attests to this.

The religion that attempts to drive a wedge between the whole realm of Faith and the actual textures of physical life is a religion that has perhaps not granted to the Incarnation the full extent of the mysteries that attach to it and flow from it, and that make our mortal life fruitful once more.

3

Christian Worship: Act or Experience?

Fifteen years after my visit to my friend's church, I found myself living in England. The natural thing was to attend the Church of England, and happily for me there was an evangelical one nearby. It was dedicated to the apostle Andrew, as churches I had known were dedicated to men like Moody or Adoniram Judson. This church honored the same gospel that my church at home had honored and spoke our language and kept in touch with the same mission organizations that we had supported. They understood the Scriptures and held the Faith in a manner virtually indistinguishable from all that I had known all my life. I was at home.

But St. Andrew's Church had been built eight hundred years ago, I was told. This datum had an effect on me; it opened my imagination backward into history. I could not kneel on the same stones where Christians had been kneeling for eight centuries and stay trapped in recent history. I knew that the first Christians to use this building had knelt for the Mass and that the Reformation had changed all of that. Nonetheless, there was a history here and even a continuum. The mysteries of the gospel had been proclaimed and celebrated here during all these centuries.

I had always had some sense of Christian history, thanks to my father. The figures who loomed the largest in my own imagination were men like Spurgeon, D. L. Moody, Hudson Taylor, and, somewhat further back, Charles Simeon, John and Charles Wesley, George Whitefield, and eventually Calvin and Luther. Before them there was a blank until I came to the apostles, who were almost as remote as Hercules or Zeus, since they existed in a sort of "holy" history. The lonely figures of Augustine and Bernard of Clairvaux (because he had written "Jesus, The Very Thought of Thee") stood in solitude in the fifteen hundred years that lay between the apostles and the Reformers.

Here, suddenly, I was hailed with a somewhat more crowded picture. I had never been to any church dedicated to "Saint" Anybody, for a start. Furthermore, there was nothing strange to these evangelicals about the fact that the roster of priests who had served this church went straight back across the Reformation to include Catholic priests. The present clergy and congregation were altogether Protestant in their own piety and doctrine, but this *link* was there. An immense antiquity stretched backward. The very stones, ancient and moss-covered, seemed to hold that antiquity and to present it to us, silently, without striving. (Some years later I was vastly impressed to hear the Bishop of Norwich, himself an evangelical of the most fervent order, thank God in his prayers for his twelfth-century predecessor, Herbert de Losinga. He acknowledged a lineage and a responsibility.)

A Position for Prayer

The first thing that struck me about this church was that the people knelt. They knelt to pray when they first came into their pews, and they knelt for all of the prayers during the service.

I myself had always desperately wanted to kneel in church. Most American evangelicals did not do that, however; so I had attempted a compromise at one point in my life, striking a somewhat stiff semi-kneel by sitting forward in the pew with my forehead on my hand, grasping the back of the pew in front, my knees angled down toward the floor but not quite touching it. I had seen dowagers do this in the Congregational

Church (very modernist) that we attended in the summers in New Hampshire, and I thought it looked more reverent, or at least more elegant, than the stolid sitting posture that most evangelicals maintain for prayer.

But here were my own evangelicals, kneeling. What joy. I could kneel with impunity.

An open-minded evangelical from one of the free-churches in America that do not kneel may read the account of a trivial matter like this and say, "Fine. If the lad wants to kneel, by all means let him. It's a very fine posture. And no doubt there is something to be said for such a practice in the Church. Certainly we free-churchmen have much to learn about reverence in worship from the ancient churches."

A response like this is a charitable one, but under the ensign of broad-mindedness it may be missing a point. It is not quite a trivial matter of mere taste or whim. To treat it so is to fall into the error of supposing that physical attitudes do not matter. It is once again to locate faith and piety in a disembodied realm. We know that this is false. Our innermost attitudes cry out for a shape. They long to be clothed with flesh. We can see this wherever we turn: we are happy and our face muscles stretch into smiles; we are sad, and our tear ducts go to work; we are ashamed, and our neck muscles incline our heads forward; we are awed, and our mouths gape open; we are exasperated, and we throw up our hands; we are angry, and we clench our fists.

We might discipline ourselves to quell all of these motions so that, like a superannuated Tibetan lama, we could sit, petrified and inscrutable, registering nothing. The lama, however, would tell us that posture matters infinitely and that it had taken him years of discipline to reach this impassivity, one of the most rigorous exercises being learning to stay motionless. The motionlessness of his body had percolated inwards and assisted his soul to be motionless.

This last point is perhaps the one that might escape us. The question is not merely one of outward gestures and postures that *express* something interior. It works the other way around as well. The outward posture actually helps to create the inner attitude. We all know this from our Sunday school teachers who told us that if we could not quite feel love for somebody, at least we should act as though we love him. The external attempt would eventually have its effect on how we feel. Baron von Hügel remarked that he kissed his son because he loved him but that he also kissed his son *in order that he might* love him. The act dragooned his somewhat untrustworthy and wayward feelings and helped to bundle them along toward their true object.

All of this raises the question, however, as to whether kneeling is an absolute for prayer.

No. For one thing, we mortals know that some of our best praying occurs at excessively awkward moments. We find ourselves squeezed in a subway, or marooned in a traffic jam, or jogging, and we realize we might as well say our prayers as waste the time. For another, if we want to adopt the most ancient posture for prayer, we will stand, probably with our hands raised. As far as we know, this was the posture in the early Church for corporate prayer.

It cannot be argued, then, that we *must* kneel. But it can indeed be argued that posture is immensely significant and that if we find shallowness to be a problem in worship services then it may be worth considering the matter. We sit for a thousand things—to eat, to chat, to work, to write notes, to rest. It may be that our bodies cry out for an attitude that will pluck us by the sleeve, as it were, and assist our inner-beings in the extremely difficult task of prayer. If in any church the sitting posture exists only as a protest against kneeling because enemy Christians kneel, then what we have is protest carried to its most dismal and barren end.

In any event, I found the practice of kneeling to be a vast relief. But it turned out to be more than a matter of what I myself might like or even what might assist us all in the act of prayer. It presently began to lodge itself in my awareness that an entirely different notion of worship was at work here from any I had ever come upon.

I had been accustomed to hearing people speak of the blessings that they had received from a given service. One spoke of what one had "gotten out" of such and such a sermon or meeting. If things were especially impressive you might even hear the phrase "a beautiful worship experience." Returning tourists sometimes told of being in Westminster Abbey or King's College Chapel at Cambridge and of finding themselves overwhelmed by the beauty of the music and the solemnity of the liturgy and the general atmosphere of reverence and dignity. It had been a beautiful worship experience for them.

From Attitude to Act

The phrase *worship experience* missed the point. Worship, in the ancient tradition, was not thought of as an experience at all; it was an act. Or, if there was an experience, that part of it was a mere corollary to the main point. At St. Andrew's the people had come together *to make the act of worship*. They had come to *do* something, not to get something. They had not come to a meeting.

Several things testified to this. For a start, no one spoke of the church "auditorium," as though it were a place one went to hear something. It was not an auditorium. Meetings did not occur here; an act occurred here. Furthermore, the vicar hardly ever addressed the congregation directly during the act of worship. Most of the time he could be seen kneeling at a small *prie-dieu* to one side of the chancel (the section of the church at the front, narrower than the nave and up some steps, that lies between the nave and the altar), facing across the front of the church, sideways to the congregation. He did not greet us, and he did not smile at us. No attempt was made to create a feeling of familiarity or welcome. And yet it was a vastly warm and friendly church. There was nothing cold or stiff there at all. These people were evangelicals.

Clearly, whatever it was that was happening did not depend in the smallest degree on atmosphere nor on the minister's establishing any sort of contact with the congregation. The notion of group dynamics would have seemed grotesque, irrelevant, and embarrassing. We in the congregation were not auditors, nor spectators, nor recipients.

We had come to this place to offer something to God, namely, the sacrifice of praise. I came to realize that there was more than a mere difference in phraseology between this and what I had always thought of as worship. There was a difference in vision.

The vicar would begin with a scriptural bidding, directing our attention to the Most High. So far all was smooth sailing for me. I was familiar with this approach. But then he would say, "The Lord be with you," and we would respond, "And with thy spirit."

What was this rote formula? I wondered. It was an exchange that occurred again and again during the service. It seemed quaint at best and possibly gratuitous; the Lord is already with both of our spirits. Why this vocal wish for the obvious?

What I did not know was that this was a formula that reaches back certainly to the beginnings of Christian worship and possibly further. It builds into the very structure of the act of worship itself the glorious antiphons of charity that ring back and forth in heaven and all across the cosmos, among all the creatures of God. It is charity, greeting the other and wishing that other one well. In its antiphonal ("responsive") character it echoes the very rhythms of heaven. Deep calls to deep. Day answers to night. Mountain calls to valley. One angel calls to another. Love greets love. The place of God's dwelling rings with these joyful antiphons of charity. Hell hates this. It can only hiss, *Out of my way, fool.* But heaven says, *The Lord be with you.* This is what was said to us in the Incarnation. This is what the Divine Love always says.

In the act of worship we on earth begin to learn the script of heaven. The phraseology has very little to do with how we may be feeling at the moment. It does not spring from us spontaneously. We must learn to say it. It is unnatural for us, the way learning a polite greeting is unnatural for a child. But to the objection that we should leave the child to express himself in his own way we would all point out the obvious, that that sort of naturalness and spontaneity is a poor, poor thing and that the discipline of learning something *else* is both an enrichment and a liberation.

Antiphony deepens the shallow pool of our personal resources and sets us free from the prison of our own meager capacity to respond adequately in a given situation. Rather than mumbling fitfully, we learn to say the formula, "How do you do?" or "The Lord be with you," and having learned it, we have stepped from solipsism into community. We have begun to take our appointed places among other selves.

In Spirit and in Truth

Reflecting on this, I felt that the distrust of rigid forms of worship might spring from innocence if not from ignorance. Those who kept insisting that "the liberty of the Spirit" stood over against such forms were forgetting the architecture of the universe. The liberating Spirit who brooded over chaos brought an exact, elegant, and mathematical order out of that chaos, and it was good. It was beautiful and free and ample. That same liberating Spirit rushed down onto the Church at Pentecost and forged that random little band of individuals into a disciplined cadre that proved invincible against the whole might of the Roman Empire.

Clearly, to pit the liberty of the Spirit against set forms is to insist on a false distinction. In response to the fear that things become rote, we may omit theorizing and ask for plain testimony from Christians who, decade after decade, repeat the same formulas. We will find from them that the formulas stay alive and salutary and that the set forms weather the passing of years somewhat better than the attempts at spontaneity, which themselves inevitably fall into rote that has the added disadvantage of being bad syntax and uncertain sentiment.

I myself would have argued for extempore prayers, for example, since set prayers were by definition automatic, and hence dead, I thought. What I was forgetting was that the extempore prayers that I knew so well were themselves made up of stock phrases strung together. I could write one here: "Our dear heavenly Father, we just want to praise and thank Thee for all Thy many blessings to us. We pray that Thou wilt give us journey mercies and that all Thy mercies, which are new every morning and fresh every evening, will be with us. We ask it in Jesus' name, Amen." All of these phrases were common currency. One heard this or heard brave, if labored, attempts to break away from these tags and be original.

No one may mock another's form of prayer. Extempore prayers and set prayers both reach the Throne if there is any spark of desire in the one praying that they do so. God is not a literary critic or a speech teacher. He does not grade our prayers. But it is for us to realize that there is great help available for us in our prayers. Spontaneity is impossible sooner or later; there only remains for us to choose which set of phrases we will make our own. The prayers of the Church lead us into regions that, left to our own resources, we might never have imagined. Also in this connection, it is worthwhile remembering that prayer is as much a matter of our learning to pray what we ought to pray as it is expressing what we feel at given moments. The prayers of the Church give us great help here.

At St. Andrew's I encountered these set prayers. After the greeting and response, the vicar would say, "Let us pray," at which point we would all kneel. He would then read a one-sentence prayer known as a collect (pronounced *col*-lect, not col*lect*).

There is a collect for every Sunday of the year in the *Book of Common Prayer* as well as for many other occasions. Here is a sample: "O God, who declarest thy almighty power chiefly in showing mercy and pity; Mercifully grant unto us such a measure of thy grace, that we, running the way of thy commandments, may obtain thy gracious promises, and be made partakers of thy heavenly treasure; through Jesus Christ our Lord." Here is another: "Let they merciful ears, O Lord, be open to the prayers of thy humble servants; and, that they may obtain their petitions, make them to ask such things as shall please thee."

Perhaps the best known of all Anglican collects is the collect for peace. "O God, who art the author of peace and lover of concord, in knowledge of whom standeth our eternal life, whose service is perfect freedom; Defend us thy humble servants in all assaults of our enemies; that we, surely trusting in thy defense, may not fear the power of any adversaries, through the might of Jesus Christ our Lord, Amen."

My distrust of such set forms was alleviated when I realized that I was already familiar with a similar phenomenon from my own church background. We had used hymns and psalms to assist us in worship, and they, like written prayers, were precast forms. We borrowed words from someone else when we used them, and, far from finding that this hampered the liberty of the Spirit, we found that our own capacity to give utterance to what was in our hearts was vastly enlarged.

The exercise held before us something to which we did not, as I recall, pay much attention, namely, the corporate nature of the Church. Most of the teaching that I remember stressed one's own spiritual life. The heavy emphasis on personal Bible reading and personal testimony spurred us to individual vigor; but the great and ancient mystery of the Church was not a major thrust of this teaching, and hence, we had little appreciation for the whole Church as a praying body, with its own prayers suitable for perpetual use.

In hymn-singing and the reading of psalms, we acknowledged the principle, of course, that we were drawing on others' words and making them our own. We would have acknowledged Charles Wesley and Isaac Watts as gifts to the Church, I think, but that is as far as the idea went. The notion of the Church itself did not reach much further than the rather diffuse idea of "the invisible Church," which meant simply all Christians always and everywhere, or else the local assembly. Prayers for the Church itself to use would have seemed a somewhat odd notion to us.

To Remit and Retain

After the collect, the vicar would say the bidding: "Let us humbly confess our sins unto Almighty God," or a similar, much longer, bidding. Then came the famous General Confession, with its widely-known phrases, "We have left undone those things which we ought to have done; And we have done those things which we ought not to have done; And there is no health in us. But thou, O Lord, have mercy upon us, miserable offenders...." At the end of this the vicar would say the Prayer of Absolution.

The very word *absolution* gave me pause. It conjured tales of priests wielding the tyranny of the confessional over terrified women. No one but God can forgive sins, we would have objected.

If we had stopped to read the Prayer of Absolution, we would have discovered that this is precisely what is counted upon in this prayer. It is God who forgives sins. The minister's is the voice we hear reminding us of this and declaring it to us. It lifts the whole transaction away from the broil of our own guilty consciences, so hard to pacify, and places it in the context of the Church, which is the Body of Christ and hence shares Christ's priestly ministry. It is here that we receive audible assurance of what we know to be true, namely, that our sins are indeed forgiven. In our private prayers we find ourselves raking back through things in uncertainty. Here the declaration is loud and clear and without doubt.

The Praying of the Psalms

Then, in another lovely antiphonal exchange, minister and people said, "Praise ye the Lord," "The Lord's name be praised." At St. Andrew's this exchange was sung, or rather chanted, as were all of the canticles and psalms.

If someone had asked me ahead of time about chant, I would, I think, have had an objection ready. Chant is analogous to Tibetan prayer wheels. The heathen chant. A chant is a monotonous, artificial, repetitious sequence of notes imposed on a text. It has the net effect of throttling whatever life there might have been in the text to begin with.

But here were evangelicals chanting! And not only that, I discovered that the chant tunes were beautiful beyond anything I had ever dreamed. They were extremely simple tunes, and indeed they were repetitious. A great number of words might be sung on one note before you moved on to the next. But the effect, far from throttling the texts, lifted them into what seemed the joyful solemnity of heaven itself. To the objection that to impose a rigorous meter and melody on biblical texts was to slay them, these people would have pointed us to hymns. There one finds highly stylized words set to rigorous melodies in exact meters. But all of us find that somehow the life of the words is thereby enhanced, not quelled. The structure is the midwife, so to speak.

Chant carries this phenomenon a step further than ordinary hymns do. It eschews the great sweep of melody available to hymns. Its thrift is its genius. Like a very simple frame around a picture, or an almost invisible setting for a diamond, it sets the text up and permits it to speak, or rather, to sing. The psalms, after all, were made for singing. Scottish meter is one way of perpetuating this, but it carries Hebrew poetry into the modern idiom of iambic tetrameter and trimeter. Chant, on the other hand, stays somewhat closer to the genius of the Hebrew, which depended on balance and repetition for its effect.

Gregorian chant, which is infinitely more austere even than

the Anglican chant that I learned to sing at St. Andrew's, carries things even further. To an untrained ear it sounds artificial in the extreme, and so it is. But artifice is a very noble thing. God Himself appointed artificers and craftsmen to make cunning things for His own Tabernacle. Real craftsmanship, far from doing violence to them, works the materials so that their own properties are released. Gregorian chant, in its subtle austerity, performs this service for biblical texts. Whereas we commonly hear them read aloud by an individual who invests the words and phrases with his own rhetorical interpretation, high-blown or understated, allegretto or largo, Gregorian chant lifts the texts away from this private milieu and arrays them, simply, out there, where we may encounter them the way we see the stars glittering on a clear night or hear the music of Bach, so utterly satisfying to our deepest imaginings.

Chant belongs to the public, not the private, order of things. Very few Christians will want to chant their private prayers, and this is as it should be.

Beyond Mere Fellowship

In the public order we are delivered from the small confines of our own breasts. We do not want intimacy here. The attempt to make public worship personal, intimate, and informal is misbegotten. It confuses the public with the private, and in so doing it betrays both.

The public is more than the collective. My recollection of public worship from my childhood is that at best it may be said to have been collective. A familiar note was struck; friendliness was important; even some jokes were admissible. Certainly we were all encouraged to do our best to concentrate on our own hearts and see that we got a blessing. There was little recognition, it seems to me, of an actual, qualitative distinction between public acts and private devotion.

I find it hard to suppose, however, that God would assign lower marks to my childhood church than He would to St. Andrew's. But public worship, like the Sabbath itself, was made for us, not us for it. It seems a pity for us to struggle along with a sort of amalgam, cobbling up worship packages and programs with a view to meeting the "needs" of a collection of people.

The worship of the Church is an act—a most ancient and noble mystery—and almost nothing is gained by endlessly updating it, streamlining it, personalizing it, and altering it. The "ministers of worship" retained on the staffs of big churches have their work already done for them if they only knew it. Worship is not something like an automotive engine or a computer, which can be perpetually improved upon. Like marriage and family, it stands at the center of the carousel of life, if we will only return to the center and find it. Insofar as we move towards the circumference of things, we will find ourselves going faster and faster.

The actual chants that we sang at St. Andrew's altered my whole vision, I think. Every Sunday we sang the *Venite* (pronounced ve-*nighty*). "O Come, let us sing unto the Lord: let us heartily rejoice in the strength of our salvation. Let us come before his presence with thanksgiving: and shew ourselves glad in him with Psalms." It is a psalm of pure praise. (In those days in England, they forged straight on through to the bitter end of that psalm, however, with "Forty years long was I grieved with this generation, and said: It is a people that do err in their hearts, for they have not known my ways...." I never found out why this grim half of the psalm had been retained as part of what was presumably to be used as an act of praise.)

Periodically we sang the great chant, *Benedicite, omnia opera Domini*: "O all ye Works of the Lord, bless ye the Lord: praise him, and magnify him for ever." From any practical or scientific point of view, the whole thing is nonsense. On and on and on it goes, verse after verse, calling upon everything imaginable, animate and inanimate, with "Bless ye the Lord: praise him and magnify him forever," repeated innumerable times.

To someone in a hurry, the repetition would be insupportable. The list is endless: Angels, Heavens, Waters, Powers, Sun and Moon, Stars, Showers and Dew, Winds, Fire and Heat, Winter and Summer, Dews and Frosts, Frost and Cold, Ice and Snow, Nights and Days, Light and Darkness, Lightnings and Clouds, Mountains and Hills, Green Things, Wells, Seas and Floods, Whales, Fowls, Beasts and Cattle, Children of Men, Israel, Priests, Servants, Spirits and Souls of the Righteous, holy and humble Men of heart—and even Daniels' three friends, Ananias, Azarias, and Misael.

This canticle takes us into very strange regions, remote from anything that our schoolbooks tell us of. All Christians believe generally that the Creation praises God in the sense that it exhibits His handiwork and rouses us to extol Him. But this canticle assumes more than this. It calls upon fire itself and frost itself to praise the Lord. If we dismiss the sentiment as metaphor or as mere Hebrew poetic convention, what are we saying? That these things are inert after all and do not praise the Lord?

If we say this, we admit to having succumbed to the lethal mythology of an era that dins into us, until we can hear nothing else, that the universe is a system. But this is not biblical language. The morning stars singing, the stars fighting against Sisera, the sun hiding its face at the Crucifixion, the rocks splitting, the floods clapping their hands, and the seas fleeing at the presence of the Lord: if we may dismiss it all as unscientific (and thereby naive and false), then we know more than the biblical writers did, and we disassociate ourselves from them. But in Christian worship we take our place in their progeny, keeping alive the vision of things as dancing in The Great Dance, and as singing "*Laudate et superexaltate eum in saeculo.*"

Evangelicalism predisposed me to embrace this vision, since it taught me to place the Bible above all other wisdom. But its frame of mind was a practical one that did not run along the visionary channels where frost praises God. Its public worship was modest and earnest; we would have been somewhat non-plussed if anyone had suggested we sing "*Benedicite, omnia opera Domini*," even in English. To this extent, surely we drew the map too small. Surely we failed to nourish a vision of things that saw the thunderous canopy of plenitude arching always over us.

Evangelical and More

The other canticle that had an unmistakable effect on my vision was the *Te Deum*. It is a hymn of undiluted praise, very widely (but probably mistakenly) attributed to Saints Ambrose and Augustine on the occasion of Augustine's baptism. It strikes a note like a tuning-fork, against which all Christian praise may test itself. It stands beyond testimony, and beyond personal experience, and even beyond thankfulness for God's blessings. It addresses God and adores Him for nothing other than His glory.

We praise thee, O God: we acknowledge thee to be the
   Lord.
All the earth doth worship thee: the Father everlasting.
To thee all Angels cry aloud: the Heavens, and all the
   Powers therein.
To thee Cherubin, and Seraphin: continually do cry.
Holy, Holy, Holy: Lord God of Sabaoth;
Heaven and earth are full of the Majesty: of thy Glory.
The glorious company of the Apostles: praise thee.
The goodly fellowship of the Prophets: praise thee.
The noble army of Martyrs: praise thee.
The holy Church throughout all the world: doth
   acknowledge thee;
The Father: of an infinite Majesty;
Thine honourable, true: and only Son;
Also the Holy Ghost: the Comforter.
Thou art the King of Glory: O Christ.

Thou art the everlasting Son: of the Father.
When thou tookest upon thee to deliver man: thou
   didst not abhor the Virgin's womb.

On and on it goes, in phrases of almost insupportable majesty, bringing to a sharp focus exactly what worship is. In the precincts to which this canticle brings us, we find that all notions of worship as being a program or a meeting have fallen away. All notions of "sharing," or even of getting a blessing, have been set aside. Now we address ourselves directly to the Sapphire Throne. What shall we say? What words shall we bring with us? Our own tongues, left to themselves, stammer, lisp, and mumble into silence.

To be sure, the Father loves that stammering and lisping as much as He does the exalted strains of the *Te Deum* set to music by Gabrielli and sung by a trained choir with brass, timpani, and incense. But the hymn is there to help us, not God. The words, coming from immemorial antiquity in the Church and sung in the Church for centuries upon end, articulate what we can only grope to say. It is a mere cavil that objects that this sort of thing is "highbrow." It has nothing to do with brows, or with taste, or anything else. Only a sorry provincialism actually insists on camp-meeting songs, folk songs, or songs of personal testimony over the *Te Deum* because these songs are somehow more "relevant." Relevance itself, in this light, becomes a pitiable thing. What is the touchstone of relevance: subjective sentiments or seventeen centuries of Christian worship?

The language in the *Te Deum* that refers to apostles, prophets, and martyrs opened up a vista for me. As an evangelical, I was aware of these figures, but I do not think I had a very lively sense of our worship now as being one with theirs. I doubt if I had thought much about them in connection with what we did on Sunday mornings in our church. The apostles and prophets were in the Bible, to be sure, and as such formed part of the story. The martyrs were somewhat suspect, having been pre-empted by the Catholic church.

The notion of ourselves, down in our little church, actually joining the chorus of adoration as it is sung in heaven, would have seemed especially vaporous to me. I had never heard the idea, taught in the Church for centuries, that in the act of Christian worship the scrim that hangs between earth and heaven is drawn back, and we in very truth join with angels and archangels and all the company of heaven who forever laud and magnify the Divine Name. It is an awesome picture of things, and it seems to be true. Evangelicalism had instilled in me a robust supernaturalism, so that I had no trouble, as a liberal Christian might, over this unabashedly apocalyptic language. It was, rather, that no one had ever bothered to open up the vision.

The invoking of that train of apostles, prophets, and martyrs also awakened in me a notion that would be theoretically affirmed by evangelicalism but which is not often dwelt on and is certainly not vivified in public worship. It is the notion of the unbroken train of the faithful on pilgrimage to the Mount of God, moving in a dazzling procession through history. In evangelicalism we had our own heroes of the faith, certainly. But the host of apostles, evangelists, fathers, martyrs, confessors, doctors, bishops, widows, virgins, and infants, recalled in so much ancient Christian hymnody and piety, was not really very present to us. The stress on our roots as going no deeper than the nineteenth century, or if we wished to go as far as the Reformation, the sixteenth, made it difficult for us to credit the ancient lineage of the faithful, even though we would have agreed that at least some faithful had been there all along.

It is more than a mere matter of sentiment. Surely one great antidote to the frantic efforts in our time, even in evangelicalism, to align Christianity's apparently uncompromising moral absolutes with the insights of psychology and "the realities of the modern world" (as though something new has come along in our century) would be to hold up once more for our gaze this train of the faithful who have held to those absolutes through thick and thin. The well-meant effort to find the outer-most borders of Christian morality and the nervous pecking at Scripture to see if we may not, after all, redraft things and bring them into line with new sexual codes are the activities of people who have been deracinated. Their roots in history have been pulled up, and they are left with nothing but the Bible and the modern world. They forget that the Faith has been borne on human shoulders and in human hearts for two thousand years.

Evangelicalism, stalwart as it is, had in effect left me with nothing but the Bible and the modern world. "*Sola Scriptura!*" we cried. But it is not *sola scriptura*. This is to ignore, with almost unpardonable hubris, the Church, full of the Holy Ghost, moving faithfully along through history. It is to pit the Bible against the Church, which is heresy. I was so fearful of the notion of "the saints" except as referring to saved souls in heaven, that I would have shunned every attempt of anyone to encourage me with the lives of people like Perpetua and Felicitas, or Boris and Gleb, or Cyril and Methodius, or Cosmas and Damian, or Martin of Tours, or Ninian, or Boniface, or Vincent de Paul.

Doctrinally, of course, evangelicalism may reply here and defend itself. But I am speaking of the shape of piety as it came to me. I am speaking of the net effect in my imagination of evangelical teaching. I can remember once coming upon the hymn, "Art thou weary, art thou languid," in an old hymn-book. It was at my mother's bidding; she told me that her mother had loved it and that I might find it helpful. After speaking for six exquisite verses about the difficulties of following Jesus, the hymn concludes, "Finding, following, keeping, struggling/Is he sure to bless?/Angels, martyrs, prophets, virgins/Answer, Yes." I was overwhelmed by this picture. What solace! What encouragement! I was in an ancient lineage, and all of these forerunners knew everything I had experienced, and all of them would testify, "Keep going! It is worth it! Praise God!"

Evangelical doctrine is correct, but there are immense treasures that it seldom dips into for the sake of its people. We were encouraged to read Christian biography, but mention of the train of the faithful did not form an organic part of worship for us, nor of our piety.

Attire

One further memory of St. Andrew's Church remains with me as having presented something new to my gaze. The vicar wore vestments or, to be technically correct, "choir habit." These were neither the richly brocaded sacerdotal vestments that I was to encounter much later nor the academic robes of Geneva worn by Presbyterians. The garb consisted of a black cassock and, worn over this, a long, rather full, white garment called a surplice. Around his neck the vicar wore a "scarf," which was a wide black length of cloth, its two ends hanging straight down the front almost to the hem of the surplice, near his ankles.

I was aware that clergy put on all sorts of garb, but I had associated it all either with Catholic priests or with modernist Protestants. I was accustomed to our own minister, who presided from the pulpit in mufti. Fortunately for us all, his taste in clothes was reasonable, so no one had to suffer through terrible neckties and worse shirts. But here was an evangelical in cassock, surplice, and scarf.

It seems pettifogging even to mention a detail like this. And we may be sure that God has no view at all in the matter. But it lodged something in my imagination that made sense. It was of a piece with the rest of what I was encountering at St. Andrew's. It had something to do with things' being impersonal.

This is a cold word. It seems almost synonymous with *heartless* to evangelicals, so accustomed are we to the personal touch and group dynamics, the informality and friendliness, of many of our churches. But there is a very rich lode to be mined here, and it goes deep into what and who we are.

Here is one way of putting the matter. When we come together in the special act of Christian worship, we long to be delivered from all that is random and chatty and fortuitous. It is not John Smith whom we need up front there, with all that he may bring of friendliness and sympathy and earnestness. We are not here for a meeting. We have had fellowship, and we have had testimonies, and we have met in each others' houses and shared our joys, griefs, and problems. Now we return to the center, to this act in which the Church appears most clearly for what it is. Now we are "the faithful," and he, whoever he may be (and it is altogether irrelevant), is "the minister." This is truer, and more profound, than that we are Tom, Dick, and Harry, or Mabel, Ruby, and Crystal. There is a sacred and liberating anonymity here. I am not primarily conscious of my own agenda of troubles now. I am a Christian, bringing the sacrifice of adoration to the Most High, as all other Christians have done before me. It does not mean that I may pretend to ignore my troubles or the troubles of others. Indeed, those burdens form part of the offering that we lift to the Throne. But our attention is now on God Himself.

For this reason, the less individuality we have to cope with in the minister, the better. His taste in clothes, his syntax, his personality—these are all very fine things. But not here. Here they only create a diversion. It was not for nothing that the priests in Israel were dressed as they were. Their garments were symbolic, to be sure, but they also cloaked the oddities that made Aaron Aaron, or Levi Levi.

This is a small point and not one that any Christian may quarrel with another Christian about. But it touches, as do all the details of anyone's customs, on matters that go deeper than the surface.

I owe thanks to St. Andrew's Church for permitting me to participate in worship as that act has been practiced by the Church for centuries. I had not known that a "worship service" was more than a meeting. I had not known that it was more than an "experience." I had never seen it very clearly as being carried on under a canopy of glory, as it were. Nothing in the public customs that I had known had pointed very far in this direction. I had not heard the old notion that the scrim between earth and heaven is drawn back during the Church's worship and that we with the liturgy, may say, and mean, "Therefore with Angels and Archangels, and with all the company of heaven, we laud and magnify thy glorious Name; evermore praising thee, and saying, Holy, holy, holy, Lord God of hosts, heaven and earth are full of Thy glory: Glory be to thee, O Lord most High."

4

Prayer: Random or Disciplined?

I remained in England for two years.

When I came back to America, I took up graduate studies at the University of Illinois. There was a small chapel across the street from the library, and I began going there daily for the service, or "Office" as it was called, of Evening Prayer.

The chapel looks something like a very tiny cathedral that has never been finished. There is no spire and no towers on the west front and no transept or apse. But the structure is tall and slender and graceful, made of gray stone in the "gothic" tradition. Like the church I had visited with my friend many years before, it spoke clearly, simply, and eloquently of the gospel mysteries in all of its design and its furnishings. Here was no "plant," built primarily for meetings and activities, announcing to the world that the great doctor so-and-so was a vastly successful money-raiser and that here was a powerhouse of activity. The building was a sort of icon. It drew one's attention to the gospel.

All buildings are icons. They all bespeak something. The spare simplicity of a clapboard New England church speaks of the demure austerity and purity that should mark the Christian's heart and, hence, the Christian's mode of life. The World Trade Center speaks of power and commerce and money. The Taj Mahal evinces the delicate, almost weightless, grace of a beautiful woman and of a man's love for her. A Cape Cod cottage with its gray shingles and white trim conjures a world that is neat, civilized, salty, and well-weathered. We cannot put a roof on four walls without making a statement.

Although I myself had always loved the great cathedrals of Europe, as most tourists try to do, I looked on them as enormous monuments to misunderstanding. Awesome and sublime as they were, they represented an effort put into the wrong place, I felt. Those people should have been building with gold, silver, and precious stones in their *hearts*, not in their cities. It should have been their hearts, not the ribbed vaulting, rising to God.

What I had missed was that one does not cancel the other. Faith, at least as I had conceived of it, was so exclusively a matter of the inner man that it could not possibly be given a shape in the physical world except perhaps by acts of charity, although I greatly distrusted any talk of good works since that seemed somehow to controvert the doctrine of grace. All was to be unseen.

Once more, my outlook was unwittingly Buddhist or Manichaean. If reality lay in the unseen realm, then the physical realm ought to be forsworn or at least de-emphasized. Although I believed the doctrine of the Incarnation, I had not done much mulling over what it might mean. To anyone who was swept away by the great cathedrals I would have pointed out crisply that Jesus built no such edifices. In so doing, I would have ignored the overwhelming fact that, while He built no such edifices, He spoke words of such power and glory that they burned into the hearts of men and kindled all the skill and creativeness that was in them. His words did not spread a frost over human potential. They roused and vivified us and set us free to do all of our work for the glory of God, whether that work meant cups of cold water, prayers, building, baking, or typing. The Word became flesh. The word always becomes flesh. What is true in a man's heart will take on the mantle of good works, or of stone, or of gilded illuminating around the border of a manuscript, or of well-baked bread.

The distrust of beauty that lay near the sources of my vision and piety betrayed a flaw. To pit beauty against faith, or beauty against good works, or beauty against humility and simplicity was to erect false distinctions. It was to imagine that the cathedrals, for example, were monuments to overweening pride, whereas many of them were dedicated to the Virgin, who is the very image of humility. Anyone who genuinely honors the Virgin is going to have simplicity and purity always before his eyes. She is no Amazon or strumpet or harridan. She will never encourage cruelty and self-assertion and hauteur. Her obedience was her exaltation; the mystery of grace always transfigures things this way, taking the things that are nothing and calling them into glorious being. Any kings and bishops who sought their own glory under the guise of honoring the Virgin in building great cathedrals were like the rest of us, happy enough to use "the Lord's work" itself to write our names large across history.

A Place to Pray

Every day at five in the afternoon I closed my books in the English graduate reading room in the library and crossed the street to the chapel for Evening Prayer. The service took about twenty minutes. The Epistle and Gospel were read, psalms and scriptural canticles were recited, and prayers were said. It was spare in the extreme. Sometimes there were only two of us in the congregation besides the reader. There was nothing at all to appeal to any wish for pomp and ceremony. There was not even any music. There was certainly no variety. Every day followed the same pattern. Variety, apparently, was entirely irrelevant.

To someone not accustomed to disciplines like this, the picture might appear bleak. How can we go on, day after day, year after year, with the same routines? Does it not all dry up and die?

Yes, indeed it does dry up and die, if there is no taproot of life irrigating it. Just as the utter sameness of marriage dries up and dies if love departs, so will any routine. To the libertine accustomed to woman after woman, the man who returns day after day, year after year, to the same spouse, with no variety, appears unfortunate in the extreme. We must ask the man himself how things are.

He will tell us that routine is the very diagram of peace and freedom: breakfast, lunch, dinner; dawn, noonday, twilight; work, play, rest. If we can ever arrange our schedules to follow this pattern, we feel ourselves fortunate. Any Christian who prays daily will tell us that in order for the exercise to become a daily one, he had to find a time for it first of all, and then he had to order that time itself into a more or less unvarying routine. Variety is the last thing he wants here. When variety asserts itself, steadfastness flies.

My own evangelicalism, stressing as it did the "spiritual" nature of the devotional life, had lodged in me a certain distrust for repetition. Even though daily private prayers were vigorously encouraged, and even though I knew that my father pursued a most austere and unvarying routine in his own daily prayers, the notion of Christians' gathering daily to repeat set prayers and canticles, with only the scriptural texts themselves supplying any variety, would have made me uneasy. I might have had the idea that a certain earnestness, and perhaps even fervor, ought to mark such gatherings and that people should be given a chance to share their concerns and to pray spontaneously.

Sharing and spontaneous prayer are salutary, but to assert this is to say nothing to the point. What about sheer routine? What about plain habit? What about prayer that does not look to earnestness and fervor for its validity?

The fact that the Church has been pursuing disciplines like this for many centuries, and that before that the Jews had done so, and that Jesus Himself and Mary and Joseph and the disciples were accustomed to such routines, would not have carried the day, in my mind. Judaism has been supplanted for one thing; the gospel brings us out of the droning of the synagogue into liberty. As for the Church, it very early lost its Pentecostal zeal, I thought. Naturally it settled down into routines.

Overcoming Individualism

Evangelicalism, encouraging a spirit of individual responsibility before the Bible, had made it possible for me to discount centuries of Christian practice. If I could not find a passage of Scripture spelling the matter out, then I felt I could abjure it. It did not occur to me that others before me—tens of thousands and millions of them—had been trying to pray and that their experience might help me. It did not occur to me that the book of Acts and the Epistles never pretend to give a picture of the Church as it settled into the long vigil of history. Once again, the notion of *sola scriptura* fostered a pert attitude in me. I took my cues from my own Bible reading; there was no such thing as "the wisdom of the Church." It did not matter that this divine Word had been read and pondered by sage and holy men and women for two thousand years before my arrival.

What I was missing was that this "wisdom of the Church" came to nothing more than common sense and Christian obedience in learning some elementary things about prolonged Christian living. The Bible does not exist in a vacuum. It is profitable, I knew, "for doctrine, for reproof, for correction, for instruction in righteousness, that the man of God may be perfect, throughly furnished unto all good works."[10] I had memorized this text in Sunday school. But the sense in which all that doctrine and correction and instruction will take root in the Church and bear fruit in wise disciplines did not present itself to me. It was as though the Church had never really existed. It was as though the Bible had been written yesterday and I were the first man to open it.

Evangelicalism had never actually claimed this, of course. But somehow the general set of assumptions at work in its handling of the Bible left me with an impression like this.

Settling into Order

I discovered, after months of being present at Evening Prayer, hearing the Scripture, and repeating the *Magnificat* and Simeon's *Nunc Dimittis*, that, far from going dry, these texts were there, as it were, awaiting my bustling arrival at five o'clock. Like gracious tutors or wise old sages, they spoke gravely and magisterially to me, settling me, reordering my topsy-turvy priorities, and leading me once more back to the center where the human soul is at home.

"My soul doth magnify the Lord, and my spirit hath rejoiced in God my Saviour." One wants to learn to say this, but the tussle of modern life, or of life in any century for that matter, does its best to crowd this out. "For he hath regarded the lowliness of his handmaiden. For behold, from henceforth all generations shall call me blessed. For he that is mighty hath magnified me: and holy is his Name." So. This is what God our Savior does with our poor mortality. He exalts it. He magnifies it so that we may magnify Him. We sing this together with Mary.

Vistas like this awaited me at Evening Prayer. The Office did not so much stand apart from the crabbed responsibilities of my work in the library as gather them up and transfigure them. To come here was not to retreat into a shelter so much as to step into clarity. This was what life was about.

The more I thought about it, the more it seemed that once a day, far from being too often for devotion, was not enough. The monastic day, punctuated every three hours with the Office, came to make great sense to me. We in the world outside the cloister could not possibly order our lives thus, but God be thanked that there were Christians who, in behalf of all busy Christian people, did give themselves to this discipline. I had never thought of the monastic life as being vicarious in this way. I had thought that monks and nuns were in hot flight from the world. No one had ever told me anything at all about what Saint Benedict had in mind for these communities.

The Office of daily Evening Prayer taught me something that I could never have learned theoretically. I would have been able to argue down anyone who tried to tell me that the Office was a good thing. I was like all the people who know what is wrong with things like that: I knew nothing about it. The Office presented a discipline that was remote from anything I had hitherto known. If the Office itself could have replied to my burbling sureties as to what was wrong with it, or how dull it was in its repetitiousness, I think it would have said, quietly, "I have been here for many centuries. There are multitudes of holy souls who will testify in my behalf."

Private Prayers

During my graduate studies I came upon the works of a man named Lancelot Andrewes. He was bishop successively of Ely, Chichester, and Winchester during the reign of James I in England and was James's favorite preacher. His sermons are to preaching what filet mignon is to food.

Andrewes worked out for himself a system of private prayer, which he entitled *Preces Privatae* (Private Prayers). He wrote it all down for himself in Greek and then in Latin. Somewhere I came into possession of an English translation.[11]

There are many forms of prayer in the book. The part that attracted my attention was the section called "Morning Prayers for a Week." Eventually I pulled these pages carefully from the paperback edition that I owned and set them into a small black leather snap-ring notebook. I wanted to use them for my own prayers.

That was perhaps fifteen years ago. I still use them daily. What I had found to be true of the prayers at St. Andrew's Church, and then of the Office of Evening Prayer, I have found to be true here: the discipline enables; the structure frees.

For many years I had tried, intermittently, to gird up my

loins and settle into a faithful manner of daily prayer. But two difficulties always ran my efforts onto the shoals. First, sooner or later I found that I was neglecting them because I did not feel in the mood to pray. And second, when I did address myself to prayer, I found that I ran out of things to say.

I cannot pretend that Andrewes's order for private morning prayers has kept me steady from the moment I adopted it. But at least it has steered me away from those two sets of shoals. Like the worship at St. Andrew's Church and Evening Prayer at the university chapel, it has taught me that one's coming to God has nothing to do with how one feels. One simply makes the act of prayer. It is analogous to the Jews' bringing their alms and sacrifices to the temple: you do it because that is what the people of God do.

Moreover, in so doing, you discover that, far from being mere drab duty, it orders your life and undergirds it and gives it a rhythm. Any honest man will admit that prayer is indeed drab duty often, and if his inclinations are the only recourse he has to help him surmount the drabness, then things are bound to be sporadic; whereas, if he has learned to look on prayer as a plain habit, he will find that it is not so much of a struggle. He may have to struggle with the state of his soul often enough, but this will not bring his prayers to a halt since these are as objective a matter as were the turtle doves that Joseph and Mary brought to the Temple.

Of course, we do not have to have a set form of prayer in order to get into the steady habit of praying. As far as I know, my father's early morning prayers were offered extemporaneously, daily, for fifty and more years. But he was an extraordinary man. I myself found, early in the game, that I could not depend on my own resources in the matter. I have had enthusiastic friends who have urged that the Holy Ghost can keep us always fresh and eager. I daresay He can, but I know very few Christians who are kept unflaggingly fresh and eager by the Holy Ghost. What we know of Him would give us reason to suppose that He is the architect of order, and that props and helps and disciplines are His ordinary methods, just as natural processes are the forms under which He continually brings new life out of the earth from seeds.

Evangelicalism had taught me the importance of prayer and had indeed taught me to pray. It had encouraged me to pray daily. But the impression I had formed was that one was more or less on one's own here. The Holy Ghost would inspire me, and I would be able to pray. Eventually I came to learn that this general line of teaching has, fairly or unfairly, been called "enthusiasm" in the Church. The general tendency is to look for direct, personal experiences from heaven and to discount external structures and aids. Christian history has been marked by many vigorous examples of enthusiasm: the Montanists, and the Quakers, and even the Wesleyans have all been called enthusiasts, not because they were especially tumultuous, but because their teaching stressed the notion of direct communication from God to the soul, sometimes to the exclusion of more plodding and indirect techniques. If the testimony of nearly everyone I have known in evangelicalism may be at all credited, then I am not alone in having found the practice of daily prayer excessively difficult to maintain over long periods without any help.

Lancelot Andrewes supplied help to me here.

In his order for private prayers, each of the seven days of the week follows the same general sequence, but the actual words that constitute the parts of the prayer differ for each morning.

On Sunday, for example, he begins with "Through the tender compassions of our God, the Dayspring from on high hath visited us." Friday has, simply, "Early shall my prayer come before Thee." The overwhelming majority of what Andrewes includes in his order for prayer is drawn from Scripture, although he also draws on ancient Jewish texts, Greek texts from the early Church, and the writings of the Fathers. The simple opening statement for each day locates the prayer. It places it starkly before God, on a firmer footing than what is to be found in the bog of one's own immediate concerns or feelings.

Then comes an act of commemoration. In this, following the seven days of Creation, one blesses God for His acts, which are recorded in Scripture as having occurred on that day. On Sunday one blesses God for light, created on the first day: "Glory be to thee, O Lord, glory be to thee, which didst create the light and lighten the world." After enumerating a great number of the blessings that come to us by virtue of light, including "the intellectual light, that which may be known of God, what is written of the law, oracles of the prophets, melody of psalms...," Andrewes includes another first-day event, namely, the Resurrection. "By thy resurrection raise us up to newness of life...," and, finally in this act of commemoration, we find Pentecost, yet another first-day event: "Thou who on this day didst send down thy thrice holy Spirit on thy disciples: take It not withal from us, O Lord, but renew it day by day in us who supplicate thee."

It may be seen already what this does to one's prayers. It sets them on a proper footing. One does not bustle into the Divine Presence with a frantic agenda of personal concerns. One takes one's place with the morning stars who sang together, with the archangelic host of heaven, and with all the company of the faithful, doing the thing that Adam was placed in the Garden also to do, namely, to bless God. The sheer horizons of one's imagination are enlarged.

During the course of the week, still following the days of Creation, one finds oneself blessing God for the seraphim and for "waters above the heavens, vapours, exhalations, whereof rains, dew, hail, snow like wool, hoar frost as ashes... waters under the heavens for drinking, washing." Who of us left to himself remembers to bless the Lord for wash water? Or for the seraphim? On Tuesday, when God brought forth the earth from the sea, one finds meadows, herbs and flowers, wine, oil, spices, stones, metals, and minerals in the list of things for which God is to be blessed. The mechanical view of nature, which has dimmed man's vision since the seventeenth century, makes it next to impossible to think that blessing God for such things is anything other than fanciful. Such difficulty here betrays how far the world has come since Genesis, the Psalms, and Revelation.

Following this act of commemoration there occurs an act of penitence. Here the words are almost exclusively those of Scripture, ranging from the Prophets to the Epistles. Then there follows an act of deprecation in which one is obliged to name things that one *ought* to deprecate: "Swelling and heedlessness...sloth and dishonesty...every evil conceit," and so forth. On Wednesday the list is borrowed from Peter Lombard's list of the Seven Deadly Sins: pride, envy, wrath, gluttony, lechery, avarice, sloth.

Then follows an act of "comprecation," a word no longer used in English. Here one finds lists of things that one ought to put his mind to pursuing. "Grant unto me to adore thee and to worship thee in truth of spirit, in comeliness of body, in blessing of the mouth," or "to win possession of my vessel in sanctification and honor." Sometimes there is a stark list. Wednesday lists humility, mercy, patience, sobriety, purity, contentment, and the readiness of zeal.

An act of faith follows, and on most mornings this act takes the form of brief phrases that follow the order of the Nicene Creed. In other words, one is anchoring his imagination in those acts that stand as his Redemption, quite unshaken either by his own fugitive emotions or by the higgledy-piggledy nature of the circumstances in which, more often than not, one finds himself. I am almost sure that I myself would never have thought of "an act of faith" as constituting an unvarying part of my prayer life. This is followed by an act of hope, which on most mornings takes the form of a simple verse of Scripture. "My soul hath longed for thy salvation and I have a good hope because of thy word" is Friday's.

Then come the intercessions. It is difficult not to quote the entire collection for all seven days.

O Thou that art the hope of all the ends of the earth: remember all thy creation for good; O visit the world with thy compassions...O succourer of the succourless, refuge in due time of trouble: remember all that are in necessity, and need thy succour....remember, Lord, for good, all at whose hands I have received good offices....have mercy on mine enemies, Lord, as on myself and bring them unto thy heavenly kingdom, even as myself....remember, O Lord, for good, and grant mercy to all them that bear me in mind in their prayers...them that for reasonable causes give not themselves to prayer remember, Lord, as if they did pray unto Thee...have mercy on them that are in extreme necessity...as on me withal when I am in extremities...those in bitter thraldoms...for them that have none to intercede for them individually...for them that have any time been scandalized by me whether by deed or by word."

On and on it goes, covering the whole human race in all of its possible categories.

If one pauses over these categories and calls up a mental image of the people included, one finds oneself being led into paths of prayer quite unimaginable to his own unassisted resources. "Those in bitter thraldoms:" who is praying for men and women languishing in Cambodian, Cuban, or Siberian cells? "Them that have none to intercede for them individually:" who prays for the friendless old women with paper bags, muttering up and down derelict staircases in the West Forties?

Then, in Andrewes's order, one prays for the Church, with all of its bishops, priests, deacons, and others who bear responsibility. At this point I fill in the names of those who bear pastoral authority in my own church tradition, as I fill in the name of the president of the United States where Andrewes prays for the king. There is space provided, of course, for one's own family and "all I have promised to bear in mind in my prayers."

Then there is an act of blessing, in which one asks God's blessing on himself; then commendation, in which the day's work is commended to God, along with one's whole life; and then praise.

> "Blessed, praised, celebrated, magnified, exalted, glorified, hallowed be thy holy Name....Commemorated, lauded, extolled, honoured, uplifted, be my strong tower...It is very meet and right, fitting and our bounden duty in all things and for all things, at all times, in all places, every way, in every hour and country, alway, everywhere, altogether, to commemorate Thee, to worship Thee, to confess to Thee, to praise Thee, to bless, to hymn, to give thanks to Thee...whom the heavens hymn, and the heaven of heavens, the angels and all the heavenly hosts without ceasing crying one to another, and we lowly and unworthy under their feet, with them. Holy, Holy, Holy, Lord God of Sabaoth, The whole heaven and the whole earth are full of the majesty of thy glory. Blessed be the Glory of the Lord from his Place.

(All of that is only part of Sunday's act of praise.) Saturday praises God, recalling

> the all-honourable senate of the patriarchs, the ever-venerable quire of prophets, the all-illustrious company of twelve apostles and evangelists, the all-famous host of martyrs, the conclave of confessors, doctors, ascetics, the beauty of virgins [and the] sweetening of the world in infants.

The Long Obedience

Why include all of this at such unconscionable length? I think it is that this set of disciplines represented a watershed in my vision that is much higher than I yet know. I have used it for many years now, and not one line of it has begun to pall. It does not stand in the way of whatever immediate petitions or concerns I may have in my own mind on a given day that need to be brought to God. This discipline has taught me that the life of prayer, if it is to be anything more than sporadic for someone like me who cannot depend on fervor to keep going, must be as regulated and independent of ephemeral inclinations as eating and sleeping are in the physical life.

It has also taught me, or begun to teach me, that prayer is far from being a matter of just my own efforts. I stand with an innumerable company of intercessors before the Mercy Seat in behalf of all men everywhere. Prayer has gone up unceasingly from righteous men since the beginning of time, like the smoke of incense. If I cannot yet conceive of myself as being a very exemplary member of that company, I may at least aspire to be one of the men who prays daily for all men. The pictures in the Scripture of Abraham and Daniel and Joseph and Mary, bringing their sacrifices to the Lord, and of those who kept vigil like Simeon and Anna, present a company amongst which one would wish most earnestly to be found.

I owe a great debt to evangelicalism for having taught me to pray. I learned in that school that any man may pray, in any words, at any time, with anything that is on his heart. Prayer was not trapped inside of missals or precast forms. I learned something of the immediacy of prayer. I imbibed a keen sense of God's moment-by-moment presence with me.

But I have wondered whether in its stress on earnestness, and even fervor, evangelicalism has not to some extent overestimated most of us. Men like George Mueller, Hudson Taylor, and Praying Hyde were held up to us as models of prayer. But this was like holding Sylvester Stallone up to a young boy and telling him to look like that. What is he to do next? Long years of discipline lie ahead. This part of the matter is not always made clear in evangelical piety.

The interior and "spiritual" nature of evangelical vision is well-placed insofar as it insists that, when all is said and done, nothing you do is worth anything if your heart is corrupt. But insofar as it leaves the impression that the interior excludes the exterior or that to be fully spiritual is to ignore routines and disciplines and crutches in favor of sheer fervor, then evangelicalism may be said to have missed at least something about the Incarnation. For in the Incarnation the immaterial became physical. God did not subject Himself merely in a masquerade to the conditions of mortal flesh; He took those very conditions and raised them and hallowed them and glorified them.

We mortals are not angels. We cannot gaze at reality directly and unblinkingly. Evangelical piety often appears to hold up before the faithful a vision of spirituality that would be available only to angels in its ceaseless fervor. Just as we must walk whereas the angels fly, so we must pray, putting one foot in front of the other, where they may soar. If, perchance, we are vouchsafed moments of exaltation, God be praised, but that is not the pattern. That is not the quotidian. That is not the school of prayer.

I am thankful to the ancient Church for its wise and earthy awareness that we Christians need all the help we can get and for supplying us with so much in its Office and in its other forms of set prayer.

5

Hail, Blessed Virgin Mary: What Did the Angel Mean?

In 1965 I was married to a lady whose first name is Lovelace. The solitary pronoun *I* changed to *we*. All the old courtly language came alive for me: "my lady," "my gracious lady," and even the word "courtesy" itself. Suddenly these quaint notions and phrases were no longer merely quaint.

Since my "field" was English language and letters, I knew and liked the quaint phrases. But scholarship could only preserve them, the way lovely artifacts and relics are kept intact in museums and reliquaries. It could not vivify them and make them leap into vibrant life.

Marriage did this for me. Gradually, I found that lovely things that had heretofore existed as truths to be admired and defended were alive. More than that, they were alive with life in the way we mortals, as opposed to the angels, encounter it, namely, in real flesh and blood.

A Holy Estate

We may say that marriage is a spiritual union. Some marriages, because of an extraordinary mutual vocation or because of some involuntary debility, exist only as spiritual unions; they are not the pattern. They are not what we mortals imagine when we speak of marriage, much less when we enter into marriage. The "spiritual" union of these two selves, with all that this entails of personalities, capacities, inclinations, potentialities, and everything else, is sealed and given shape, nay, is effected, by being physical. The physical union is more than simply the expression of love. It assists the continuous creation of that love. It is the mode under which that love is known.

The very routines of domestic living become the bearers of significance, not as though there is now some added meaning in common activities like washing dishes, shopping, and drinking tea; but that simply by being themselves, these activities mediate the mystery to us, as it were. We are married. What does that mean? Where does the transaction exist? What is this "holy estate"? Where do our ordinary selves touch the mystery of holy matrimony?

Wherever the mystery may lodge—in my heart and Lovelace's, or in heaven, or in "the nature of things"—it takes on present actuality for us in tangible forms. The inner, spiritual bond is there, but it takes on shape and substance in physical forms. We discover this the minute we find we must be away from one another. We are just as married, spiritually, when we are a thousand miles apart. But spiritual union is not enough. We are not angels. Being near to each other matters. Touch matters. Our union exists in more than the world of thoughts.

The cups of tea together, the conversations, the coming and going that our different responsibilities ask of us, and our sleeping together all *express* the inner bond that is there, *but they also give a human shape to that bond*. We may say even more: these outward things turn out to have been transfigured—transubstantiated, so to speak—by the inner reality of sacred marriage. Now it is a cup of tea *with my spouse*. Now it is my work and hers, constituting one life.

Sexuality itself is hallowed by the sacred bond, whereas, without that bond it is profane. The same act is called by different names according to whether the inner reality is absent or present: fornication or union, charade or a reality, desecration or a holy thing.

All of us, from the peasants to the philosophers, know these things from ordinary human experience. The greater the significance of something, the more difficult it becomes to divide the inner from the outer. Put the other way around, the more profound our experience, the more we discover the seamlessness that recalls Eden to us and anticipates Paradise.

Denying the Division

A husband and wife do not have two relationships, one on the spiritual level and another on the physical. The more perfect a marriage grows, the more these two become indistinguishable. If, because of infirmity, age, or necessity of one sort or another, they are driven apart physically, they then experience something of the division between spirit and flesh that fractures all of mortal life. Marriage has been rightly perceived by all religions and cultures to be in some sense hallowed. In this strange bond we come close to that perfect wholeness for which we were made and into which we ourselves introduced division.

Christians believe, however, that God has done more about that tragic division than merely leave us with reminders, like marriage, of the oneness of spirit and flesh that marked the original Creation. They believe that in the Incarnation that oneness was restored to human life.

Other religions have their ways of coping with the division. Most of them, one way or another, set the unseen realm over against the seen and end up denigrating the latter. For them, release, or salvation, comes when we are set free from the prison of this flesh and fly away into the Aether, or the Oversoul, or the All.

Union in Christ

Christianity, on the other hand, throws up roadblocks to any such itinerary. It is heavy with physical, and even clinical, details. For thousands of years of human history, according to Christianity, the way was prepared for our salvation, not by the

Lord God's weaning men away from their physical life and teaching them to be spiritual, as the Buddha and Plato and other sages have urged. Rather, the way He laid out was crowded with altars of stone, and bloody pelts, and entrails and great haunches of lamb and beef, and gold and incense and fine-twined linen, and immense golden bulls holding up the brazen sea in the Temple. Doves, heifers, bullocks, rams—it was very crowded.

But that was all primitive. Surely something spiritual would emerge from those elementary lessons. Surely thoughtful men might anticipate the day when all of this would be put behind and be replaced with elevated thoughts and spirituality.

Indeed it was all put behind. There came an end to those gory altars and all that slaughter. But it was not a tissue of elevated thoughts that replaced them. Rather, an angel appeared to a woman and said, "Hail!" What we now had, far from the summons away from the physical realm that highminded men might have wished, was gynecology, obstetrics, and a birth. Whatever we may imagine about the spiritual rhapsody that might have attended this angelic visitation to the Virgin, the one thing we know to have occurred was a conception. The Virgin's womb teemed.

It was embarrassing to the religious mind. It proved a scandal. The whole ensuing story bothered and even enraged religious men, and it has continued to do so. Christian history is littered not only with the bones of martyrs who have died at the hands of enemies who hated this story but also with the confused and heretical attempts of Christians themselves to skirt it. Seizing on Saint Paul's vocabulary and wrenching it about, they have tried to pit the spiritual against the physical and have tried to make Christianity like Buddhism, a religion that summons us away from earthly, earthy life.

Our Own Worst Enemies

It has not only been Christianity's enemies and its heretics who have done this. Some of its stalwarts, defending with all zeal the gospel that tells of Annunciation, Visitation, Nativity, Circumcision, Purification, Temptation, Last Supper, Passion, Resurrection, and Ascension have by some unwitting alchemy managed to leave with the faithful the idea that Christian worship and devotion exist in a realm detached from the physical.

Some modes of Christian worship, for example, in reaction to the riot of superstition that bedeviled the latter Middle Ages, went to the extreme of jettisoning altogether the ancient liturgy of the Church and substituted for that liturgy a meeting or a "worship service." Gone now was the ceremonial enactment of the great events of the gospel, which kept before the eyes of the faithful, day by day, century after century, that whole drama in which the Word took on our flesh and lived our human life. Gone now was the yearly round that marked the events of His life—that sequence of Annunciation, Visitation, Nativity, Circumcision, and the rest, all so physical.

In its place came the verbal iteration of the titantic abstractions of theology: election, sovereignty, predestination, atonement, justification. Gone, in the name of an abstract grace, was the Holy Sacrament to which mortal creatures had come in faith for so many centuries to make the offering of themselves, their prayers, their adoration, and their sufferings one with the only perfect self-offering and sacrifice ever offered to the Most High, namely, that of the Lamb of God at the cross.

In the storm and stress of reform, a division had entered once again. Faith was pitted against works. The Word was pitted against Sacrament. Inner devotion was pitted against enactment. Even the Bible was pitted against the Church. *Sola Scriptura*! rang out, as though the Incarnation were a footnote to revelation and the Church itself an afterthought.

The interior was pitted against the exterior. The Christians who stressed election and atonement and justification—those thunderous mysteries of Redemption—expunged from their public observances almost all ceremonial recognition of the actual physical events to which those thunderous mysteries are always anchored. The new piety seemed to forget that revelation and redemption had not come to us only in a book.

The God who had given the Book on Sinai had, in the last times, spoken, not merely through evangelists and apostles, but in a Son, born of a virgin, circumcised, presented in the temple, tempted, slain, risen, ascended, and now offering his Body and Blood to us for our food. Our mortal life, with all of its routines, its physical conditions, its triumphs and its sufferings, was borne by this Son. He spoke to us in His teaching to be sure, but all that He said was clothed in flesh and enacted for us in His life, Passion, Resurrection, and Ascension.

For some Christians it came to seem that Pauline theology constituted the nub of revelation and that the drama of the Incarnation was a mere necessary preliminary mechanism for getting the thing done and ushering in the era of theology and spirituality. For them it became difficult to see that in the events of the gospel itself the entire drama of revelation was played out and that to keep those events always before the eyes of the faithful was the unceasing task of the Church.

I have spoken of the "ceremonial recognition" of the actual physical events of the gospel, events that in their very simplicity are freighted with rich mystery for us. I have mentioned the yearly round that marks and celebrates those events. Almost all Christians, with the exception of a few groups who refrain for conscience' sake, mark the Nativity and the Resurrection with great joy. Christmas and Easter remain as a sort of skeletal Christian year throughout Christendom.

Worshiping at St. Mary's

When Lovelace and I settled in New York, our parish church was one that maintained the ancient ceremonial worship of the Church and observed the whole Christian year with great joy. The church itself was dedicated to Saint Mary the Virgin.

In some Christian traditions churches are named after a street: Park Street, Lake Avenue, or Wealthy Street. In others, polity is honored: First Baptist, Tenth Presbyterian. In still others, a man is honoree: Moody Church, Judson Church, the Lutheran Church. In still others, some aspect of the Faith is taken as a sort of banner for the church: Calvary Church, The Bible Church, Grace Chapel. Sometimes friendliness is sought: The Church by the Side of the Road or The Church of the Open Door. Sometimes a special biblical word is taken for a name: Berachah, Bethany, Maranatha, Zion.

Most of these names would stem from comparatively recent tradition in Church history. But if we go back many centuries, we will find very much the same idea at work—that is, that it is a worthy thing to stress some aspect of the Faith or to honor some exemplary Christian in the naming of a local parish. The idea has never been that the name of the church in question excludes other aspects of the Faith, as though in Grace Chapel one never hears about good works, or in Calvary Church one never hears about the Resurrection, or in Moody Church greater honor is paid to D. L. Moody than to God. All churches belong to God and none other, but in naming their parishes, Christians have often sought some modest reminder of one aspect of the gospel.

In the ancient churches the tendency was to name the parish after something or someone important to the Faith. The cathedral in Norwich, England, for example, is named The Cathedral of the Holy and Undivided Trinity. This does not mean that it stands somehow closer to the center of things than, say, Westminister Abbey, which is dedicated to Saint Peter, even though everyone would agree that the Trinity is indeed the center. Both places would claim to teach and celebrate the whole Faith. But since we are limited mortals and cannot maintain our grasp very well on everything at once, we find that it is worth choosing a foothold, so to speak, in the immense massif of the Faith.

Some churches in the ancient tradition are named after gospel events: The Church of the Incarnation, The Nativity, The Transfiguration, The Ascension, and so forth. Some are named after apostles rather than more recent dignitaries: Saint Paul, Saint John, Saint Thomas. Some are named after figures exemplary of the Christian life, either by virtue of martyrdom or of extraordinary sanctity: Saint Polycarp, Saint Ignatius of Antioch, Saint Francis, Saint Bridget.

Many of the ancient churches were dedicated to Mary. As in the case of churches dedicated to Moody or Judson, the idea here was not to pay honor to a mortal instead of God who alone may be worshiped but, rather, to have the church stand as a perpetual witness to the Faith itself, with Mary remembered and honored as the central human figure of the Faith.

If we are speaking of the great train of all who have gone before us in the Faith—patriarchs, prophets, kings, apostles, evangelists, martyrs, fathers, doctors, confessors, bishops, virgins, widows, and infants—then Mary unquestionably stands in the place of preeminence by virtue of her unique role in the drama of Redemption. Whereas all these others bore witness to the Word, she bore the Word. In no other mortal figure do we see the mystery of Redemption so richly revealed. God took up His abode in her flesh. Nay, we may say more: God the Word received His human flesh from the gift of the Virgin. Mystery of mysteries: this divine humility that will, as Creator, receive Its very flesh from Its creature. Pattern of all charity, that will place Itself in debt to Its debtors; the Everlasting Son content to call this woman Mother, who herself was hailed by Dante as *figlia del tuo figlio*, daughter of your Son.

The Virgin is the great archetype of what God looks for when He comes to us. "Be it unto me according to thy word," she said;[12] whereas, our first parents said in effect, "Be it unto me according to *my* word." Her humility and her obedience— "Behold the handmaid of the Lord!"—are synonymous with her exaltation. "Hail!" said the angel Gabriel. "Highly favored! Blessed art thou among women."[13] Her cousin Elisabeth hailed her with a similar courtesy, awestruck that the mother of the Lord should deign to visit her.

Homage to Mary

Why all these courtesies? Was the angel inaugurating a greatly mistaken piety? Was Elisabeth overzealous? Would these greetings not seem to deflect our attention from God, who alone is to receive our worship? Has not that angelic greeting proved to be the fountainhead of a whole cult that has supplanted the worship of Christ Himself?

Millions of Christians who honor this most highly favored Lady do seem to hold her Son in an almost paralytic awe, as though He were a sultan or khan whose name must hardly be uttered, from sheer fear. Their prayers and devotions imply that she is, somehow, more gracious, more understanding, more bountiful, and more lovely than her Son. To the extent that this is true, devotion has gone awry.

The antidote has impoverished millions of other Christians. A parsimonious notion of God's glory has been one result of the revulsion felt by so many over the honor paid to Mary, as though to say, If God alone is all-glorious, then no one else is glorious at all. No exaltation may be admitted for any other creature, since this would endanger the exclusive prerogative of God.

But this is to imagine a paltry court. What king surrounds himself with warped, dwarfish, worthless creatures? The more glorious the king, the more glorious are the titles and honors he bestows. The plumes, cockades, coronets, diadems, mantles, and rosettes that deck his retinue testify to one thing alone, his own majesty and munificence. He is a very great king, to have figures of such immense dignity in his train, or even better, to have raised them to such dignity. These great lords and ladies, mantled and crowned with the highest possible honor and rank are, precisely, *his* vassals. This glittering array is his court! All glory to him and, in him, glory and honor to these others.

We know all of this from reading about the courts of great kings in our own history. We also know it of God, who is attended by creatures of such burning splendor that we can scarcely imagine them: angels, archangels, virtues, thrones, dominations, princedoms, powers, and then the terrible cherubim, and finally the seraphim themselves. Who knows what all of this is? It is the host of immortals.

This does not exhaust the court of the Lord, however. In this throng are creatures who, beyond imagination, bear a dignity excelling that of the immortals. These are the ones of whom alone it is said that they were made in God's image. This is not said even of the seraphim. What it might mean no one knows yet, but it is a dignity mantling them alone.

Even beyond this, the mantle of their flesh is the mantle taken by God Himself at His Incarnation. Most glorious mantle—no ermine, no purple, no cloth of gold, no robe of angelic light can match it.

And not only this, we are taught by the apostle Paul that these creatures, redeemed from their own fall into wretchedness, are now crowned and made to reign with Christ Himself. Glory piled upon glory. What songs will celebrate the glory of this multitude? What acclamations will answer to its splendor? Figures of immense dignity appear among them: Adam, Eve, Enoch, Abraham, Moses, Deborah, Elijah, and countless others.

The Blessed Virgin

There is one whose dignity is shared by no other. She is a woman, the humblest of them all. No empress, prophetess, or conqueror she, only the handmaid of the Lord. But in her exaltation we see the divine magnanimity, which has regarded the lowliness of His handmaiden and has exalted the humble and meek. In her we learn of God who brings to nothing the pride of the great and sends the rich away empty. "Magnificat!" she sings, and "Hail!" we answer, in the joyful courtesies of heaven.

The Christian piety that has been afraid almost to name,

much less to hail, the Virgin and to join the angel Gabriel and Elisabeth in according blessing and exaltation to her is a piety that has impoverished itself. Stalwart for the glory of God alone, it has been afraid to see the amplitude of that glory, which brims and overflows and splashes outward in a surging golden tide, gilding everything that it touches. Saint Francis had an eye for this and exulted in everything made by God, hailing even the sun and the moon and the fire as brothers and sisters, in a poetic overflow of charity. In contrast to this, the punctilious insistence that nothing be exalted and glorified except God alone begins to seem parsimonious.

We are taught by Scripture that nothing may be *worshiped* but God alone. The ancient Church has always taught this, reserving for God alone the honor known as *latria*. But, below this worship paid to the Most High, there is a whole scale of exultation and exaltation that rejoices in the plenitude of the divine glory and leaps to hail every creature in whom that glory is seen.

A Christian devotion afraid to join the angel of God in hailing the Virgin as highly exalted is a devotion cramped either by ignorance or fear.

6

Ritual and Ceremony: A Dead Hand or the Liberty of the Spirit?

In The Church of St. Mary the Virgin, my wife and I found ourselves assisting at the liturgy from week to week. "Assisting at": that is the phrase that must be used, recalling the notion among the early Christians that everyone present at Christian worship was a full participant. Bishops, priests, deacons, and laity were the four orders in the Church that we glimpse in the New Testament and in the writings of the men taught by the apostles. There were no spectators.

The idea is kept alive in the French verb *assister a*, which we translate too weakly "to be present at." But the worship of the Church, specifically its Eucharistic liturgy, is not a meeting or a program to which we come only to receive something. It is an act, to which we come as participants, indeed as celebrants, if the doctrine of the priesthood of all believers means anything.

The Work of the People

The word *liturgy*, which unfortunately dropped out of use long ago in Protestantism, spells out what Christian worship actually is. "The work of the people" is what the word means, and the early Christians used this word to refer to what they did when they came together week by week on the first day to worship God. It was not a generalized and diffuse worship that they offered up, such as we might find among highminded pagans, deists, and transcendentalists. Christian worship meant one thing: the Eucharistic liturgy. It is a measure of how much was jettisoned at the Reformation that both of these words are unfamiliar to millions of Christians, even devout Christians. The liturgy was understood by the early Christians to be their special work, and that work was the offering up of worship to God as Eucharist, that is, as thanksgiving.

Once again, it was not a merely generalized thanksgiving, appropriate as that might be as an offering for Christians to make. Rather, it was the Christians' particular offering to God of themselves, their lives, and their intercessions, thanksgivings, and adoration, in union with the only offering acceptable to Him, namely, the self-offering of the Lamb of God at the cross.

All the Old Testament offerings had anticipated this, and Old Testament worship followed the pattern given by God, a pattern which, it turned out in the fullness of time, perfectly prepared the way for the one sacrifice. In the New Testament all those old types and foreshadowings were fulfilled and hence done away with, and Christian worship took on a new form, following the pattern laid down by Christ the Lamb at the Last Supper just before His Immolation. In an act that must have bemused the disciples, He took bread and blessed it and broke it and gave it to them, saying, "This is my body." The wine He blessed and gave to them was likewise His blood, He said.

If this were all there was to it—just that brief scene from the Gospel account—we might well leave it at the margin of worship, as many churches decided to do after the sixteenth century. But we find that the early Church almost immediately took up this strange act of Christ's, and these strange words, and found in them the diagram of its worship.

Worship in New Testament Times

In the earliest glimpses that we can get of what these Chris-

tians did, we find them doing this. Saint Luke mentions in Acts
the apostles' fellowship, teaching, prayer, and the breaking of
bread. We hear of singing, preaching, and praying in other
New Testament allusions. But we never come upon an actual
description of what Christian worship consisted of until we
read of it in the writings of the men who followed the apostles,
some whom had been taught by them. Here we find the Eucharistic liturgy already in place.

Any Christian believer looking into these matters will find
himself moved. The time of liturgy was a time of great joy. Ignatius of Antioch, who was contemporary with all of the apostles, speaks of the Eucharist, as do Justin and Irenaeus and
other writers. A hymn, written perhaps while some of the
apostles themselves were still alive, expresses how the Christians saw the Eucharist and saw themselves as having been
made one with Christ's Eucharistic self-offering.

> As grain, once scattered on the hillsides,
> Was in this broken bread made one,
> So from all lands thy Church be gathered
> Into thy kingdom by thy Son.[14]

It is as though the Church, like the loaf that Christ took and
broke, has been made one from many scattered seeds and, like
bread, has no other purpose than to be broken for the life of the
world. In this picture we see something of the compression
that is present in the Eucharist; the whole mystery of the gospel inheres in this simple act. Christ, the Son of God, is also
the Bread of God, giving Himself for the life of the world, and
in so doing revealing to us what had hitherto only been intimated by the Law and the Prophets, that the Most High is
Love. (There, somehow, lies the mystery that we call the Trinity.)

This divine love is such that not only does God give Himself
to us and for us but, unimaginably, *takes us into this very mystery of self-giving and makes us one with His Son*, calling us

the very Body of this Son who offers Himself to the Father for the life of the world.

Here we find the gospel mystery, in almost impenetrable density: The bread of the Eucharist is the Body of Christ, and the Church is the Body of Christ; and that Body—both Christ's personal body conceived and nourished in the womb of the Virgin, and his Body the Church—like bread, has only one reason for being: to be broken and given. "Lo I come (in the volume of the book it is written of me) to do thy will, O God,"[15] says the writer of Hebrews, putting words into Christ's mouth, "a body hast thou prepared me," to be the sacrifice to end all sacrifices. This is what this body was for; this is what bread is for; this is what the Church His Body is for. All is offering; all is sacrifice; all is oblation.

As Old as Eden

Suddenly we find ourselves back in Eden, where things went awry when we refused the oblation of all things to God and, in the attempt to wrest them for our own, ruined everything. The Fall is the refusal of oblation; Redemption is the renewing of oblation. Put another way, the refusal of oblation lost everything; the renewing of oblation redeemed everything. What the first Adam, that is to say we ourselves, refused, the second Adam offered to the Father, namely, everything: Himself, His obedience, His thanksgiving, and His adoration. At the first Eucharist Jesus Christ *gave thanks*: the very moment of His Immolation was the moment of Eucharist.

No wonder the Church took up this name and gave it to its worship. What other name would suffice for this act? For worship without oblation is no worship. Worship that vaunts itself or that holds anything back is no worship. To worship the Most High is to give all to Him: blessing and honor and glory and power, and "our selves, our souls and bodies, to be a reasonable, holy, and living sacrifice unto thee," as the great Eucharistic prayer phrases it.

Since the liturgy both recalls these great mysteries for us and also makes them vividly present to us, it has always been a ceremonial act. A mere meeting for "the preaching of the Word" does not quite exhaust, or even answer to, the solemnity of what Christian worship actually is.

The rite that Jesus recalled at the Last Supper was the ritual *Berakoth*, the set of Jewish prayers for which the Greek translation was the word *Eucharist*.[16] He was not improvising. It was not an impromptu or extempore meal that He ate with His disciples there in the upper room. In His mind there was no conflict between ritual and "the liberty of the Spirit," in which He Himself lived in perfect freedom.

For Christians who think of ceremony and ritual as standing over against the liberty of the Spirit, the liturgy suggests a grid, or pall. Those who feel this way, and who have never actually participated in the ancient liturgy of the Church, may be helped at least to understand something of what is at work here by pondering the following remarks from C. S. Lewis.

Lewis has been speaking of the formal language that we find in epic poetry and has pointed out that it combines "specialness" with predictability and easy accessibility.

A parallel, from a different sphere, would be turkey and plum pudding on Christmas day; no one is surprised at the menu, but every one recognizes that it is not *ordinary* fare. Another parallel would be the language of a liturgy. Regular church-goers are not surprised by the service—indeed, they know a good deal of it by rote; but it is a language apart. Epic diction, Christmas fare, and the liturgy, are all examples of ritual—that is, of something set deliberately apart from daily usage, but wholly familiar within its own sphere.... Those who dislike ritual in general—ritual in any and every department of life— may be asked most earnestly to reconsider the question. It is a pattern imposed on the mere flux of our feelings by reason and will, which renders pleasures less fugitive and griefs more endurable, which hands over to the power of wise custom the task (to which the individual and his moods are so inadequate) of

worship [less]
irregard[less]
one
How
feels.

being festive or sober, gay or reverent, when we choose to be, and not at the bidding of chance.[17]

Lewis touches here on something profound, which does not always present itself easily to people like us who are keen on expressing themselves and who have been taught that freedom lies in getting rid of structures. It is an idea especially difficult for people whose religion has taught them that structures are deadening. That ritual might actually be a relief, and even a release, is almost incomprehensible to them. That the extempore and impromptu are eventually shallow, enervating, and exhausting seems a contradiction to these people, who so earnestly believe that nothing that does not spring from the authenticity of the moment is actually fruitful.

As Lewis points out in this same context: "The unexpected tires us; it also takes us longer to understand and enjoy than the expected. A line which gives the listener pause is a disaster ...because it makes him lose the next line."[18] Any Christian who has tried to stay abreast of impromptu public prayers will testify to the truth of this observation.

Ritual and Ceremony

The liturgy of the Church is made up of two elements, ritual and ceremony. Ritual refers to the words, ceremony to the actions.

The same difficulties arise over ceremony that arise over ritual. Great numbers of people suppose that ceremony is deadening and, perhaps worse, is really a matter of mere folderol, or high-jinks. They look on the liturgy of the Church as a "show." They make a very great mistake.

What is lost in this view is the nature of ceremony itself. Of course ceremony may be mere folderol. Many ceremonies are a waste of time; others are organized merely as entertainment. To point this out is hardly to have approached the topic. Ceremony lies at the taproot of what we are. We are ceremonial creatures.

To see this we need only recall a very simple thing. The more important an event or experience is for us mortals, the more we ceremonialize it. We may take the three most basic experiences of human life as illustrations: birth, mating, and death. We, like dogs, pass through all of these, but unlike dogs, we are not content merely to pass through them; we must also *do something about them.* This seems to be the mark of our humaness, and the thing which we do about these experiences is to ceremonialize them. All of them are routine, but we, being human and not merely bestial, see something in them. We see significance, and the thing that we do about significance is to reach for ceremony.

Take birth, for example. It is a merely obstetric event and has been going on in all tribes and civilizations since the beginning. Nothing could be more routine; yet we recognize that birth is something more than a mere function or routine, and we mark the event with some ceremony. When the Lamaze exercises and the dieting and the midwives and doctors have done all they can do, and the child is born; then come the ceremonies. Cigars are passed out—surely not an activity that contributes anything practical to the matter. Champagne is uncorked. Even before the event, the way has been laid out with pink, blue, and yellow, and with little ruffles stitched for the bassinet. Year after year, there are cake and candles and gifts in pretty paper to commemorate the event.

Folderol certainly, and completely nonfunctional; but nevertheless absolutely central to what we are.

Again, mating is a mere component of our animal natures, which we share with dogs. Unlike them, we recognize the physical phenomenon as vastly significant, and we set it about with ceremony. Some cultures have elaborate puberty rites; virtually all cultures have elaborate wedding rites. The coming together of the male and the female is routine and natural, but it is unique in each case; and the way we mark this uniqueness is with ceremony. Not one single one of the ceremonies that attend marriage is necessary biologically, but only the beasts suppose that the marriage is complete without them. They, and the people who attempt to make human life as close to the bestial as possible, merely copulate, but Hindus, Moslems, Jews, animists, and Christians, and everyone else except modern people know that this is a travesty and a sacrilege.

Ceremony accompanies death, as well. Long palls, drawn hearses, music, slow processions, hushed crowds, flowers, obsequies—there are a hundred ceremonies that we reach for when the pills and the X-rays and the tubes and respirators and scanners have done all they can. Of all human events, death is the most intractably physical. It is almost vegetable; we go back to the loam to decompose. But we will not leave death at that. We ceremonialize the event. We *must* ceremonialize the event.

Folderol? The dogs might think so, but human beings do not.

A Door to the Truth

Those who suppose that ceremony is simply something extra, like frosting on the cake that has little to do with the substance of things, may be asked to ponder the odd fact that every time we resort to ceremony, we do so not to escape the stark reality of the event, or to veil it, much less merely to decorate it, but to give shape to the full reality and significance of what has happened.

Ceremony assists us to cope with the otherwise unmanageable. Far from erecting a barrier between us and the truth, it ushers us closer in to the truth. It dramatizes the truth for us. *Ceremony does what words alone can never do.* It carries us beyond the merely explicit, the expository, the verbal, the propositional, the cerebral, to the center where the Dance goes on.

If this idea seems suddenly to have taken flight and to have retreated from the clear and practical world of mature and reasonable experience into metaphor and fancy, we may consider another observation that C. S. Lewis makes, this time concerning ceremony. He is speaking of the old word *solempne*.

Like *solemn* it implies the opposite of what is familiar, free and easy, or ordinary. But unlike *solemn* it does not suggest gloom, oppression, or austerity. The ball in the first act of *Romeo and Juliet* was a 'solemnity'. The feast at the beginning of *Gawain and the Green Knight* is very much of a solemnity. A great mass by Mozart or Beethoven is as much a solemnity in its hilarious *gloria* as in its poignant *crucifixus est*. Feasts are, in this sense, *more* solemn than fasts. Easter is *solempne*, Good Friday is not. The *Solempne* is the festal which is also the stately and the ceremonial, the proper occasion for *pomp*—and the very fact that *pompous* is now used only in a bad sense measures the degree to which we have lost the old idea of 'solemnity'. To recover it you must think of a court ball, or a coronation, or a victory march, as these things appear to people who *enjoy* them; in an age when every one puts on his oldest clothes to be happy in, you must re-awake the simpler state of mind in which people put on gold and scarlet to be happy in. Above all, you must be rid of the hideous idea, fruit of a widespread inferiority complex, that pomp, on the proper occasions, has any connexion with vanity or self-conceit. A celebrant approaching the altar, a princess led out by a king to dance a minuet, a general officer on a ceremonial parade, a major-domo preceding the boar's head at a Christmas feast—all these wear unusual clothes and move with calculated dignity. This does not mean that they are vain, but that they are obedient; they are obeying the *hoc age* which presides over every solemnity. The modern habit of doing ceremonial things unceremoniously is no proof of humility; rather it proves the offender's inability to forget himself in the rite, and his readiness to spoil for every one else the proper pleasure of ritual....You are to expect pomp. You are to 'assist', as the French say, at a great festal action.[19]

For Protestant Christians whose discipline, piety, spirituality, and doctrine have all been primarily verbal and interior, and, hence, whose public worship has taken the form of a meeting, these observations may help clear away some of the misgiving they have felt with respect to highly ceremonial worship. Ceremony belongs to the essential fabric of what we are. We do not need verses from the Bible to validate ceremony for us any more than we need verses to tell us to eat our meals or to have sex. The Bible is not a handbook of everything. It opens up the vision of God for us mortals, and this vision comes upon our mortal life and redeems it and transfigures it and glorifies it, so that all that we are springs into new vigor. Far from quelling our human potentialities and yearnings and capacities, it redeems them and sets them free. The question, then, is not so much "Where did all this ceremony come from?" as "How can it possibly have come about that when some Christians come to the very center of everything, they prohibit ceremony?"

To prohibit ceremony, or even to distrust it, and to reduce the worship of God Himself to the meager resources available to verbalism, is surely to have dealt Christendom a dolorous blow. To have substituted a meeting, no matter how formal it might be, with robed clergy and ministerial tones, for the ancient liturgy of the Church, is like having removed all of a man's viscera because he was covered with sores and putrescence. The surgery is too drastic.

The Drama of the Gospel

The liturgy, then, which rises from the very first years of the Church's life as it moved from the flush of Pentecost into its long, slow pilgrimage through history, combines ritual and ceremony. In so doing, it touches us deeply and exquisitely. Nay, we may say more: it calls to all that is in us and summons us not only to hear about the gospel, or to think about it, but to *enact* it. For that is what the liturgy is: the ceremonial enactment of the whole drama of the gospel.

The idea of enactment itself gives pause to many Christians. Is it not a charade? Mummery? Trumpery? Is it not to transport pretense and mime into sacred regions that ought not to be thus trivialized? All this bowing and sprinkling and turning this way and that: surely this is to have left the simple gospel and to have returned to heathendom?

The answer to this entirely worthy line of questions lies close at hand. Everything depends on what is being enacted. Enactment itself, since it is almost synonymous with ceremony, is, as we have seen, part of the very fabric of our human life. We do enact things. We will enact things. No one can stop us from enacting things. The most gaunt anti-ceremonialist may refuse to take off his hat in a shrine, whereupon he has given the whole game away. He agrees with the priests at the shrine that hats on or hats off are significant, and to register his dissociation from their cult, he keeps his on. It is a ceremonial enactment of what he believes. A church wishes to stress the table aspect of the Eucharist, so it instructs its people to remain seated as they eat the bread and drink the cup. This is a ceremonial enactment of something important to them. They agree with the Christians who kneel that posture is immensely significant. The external act matters; stay seated.

Too Much or Not Enough?

There is still, however, the possible objection that too much ceremony is a bad thing and, more serious than this, that certain acts do, in fact, look heathen. Bowing, for example: don't Buddhists and Taoists do a lot of bowing? Christians do not want to be found aping heathendom.

Again, the answer lies close at hand. Christians gathered to enact the Eucharist are no more aping the heathen when they bow at the mention of the Holy Name than any Christian is when he bows his head to say grace. Moslems bow; animists bow; we all bow. The question is only *"To Whom* am I making my obeisance?" If it is Baal or Ashtaroth, then the objection is not that I have bowed, but only that I have bowed to the wrong deity.

When it comes to the question of too much ceremony, we are on ground where no one is entirely steady. How much or how little ceremony shall we have at the birthday party? Shall we dim the dining room lights and process in from the kitchen with the cake, cueing everyone to sing as the procession arrives? Or shall we just finish the main course and reach for the cake from the sideboard, lighting the candles at the table if someone can come up with some matches? Who can answer these questions? It all depends on how much we wish our actions to answer to our sense of the joy and dignity of the occasion. Informality and randomness strike one kind of note; the procession with the dimmed lights strikes another.

The "best" ceremony, if we may put it that way, is the one that most completely unites meaning and action, the one in which what occurs on the surface answers most fully to all that is meant.

Returning to the example of a wedding, we see that many ceremonial acts occur, any of which a couple might omit and still be legally married. No bride needs bridesmaids, much less bridesmaids in fancy dresses. No bride needs a wedding dress. The slow procession takes time that might be used for other, more important things. The groom might just as easily bring her down the aisle, or they might just as easily straggle in with the congregation and then, at a given signal, leave their pews and go to the front for their vows. Rings might be dispensed with. Nothing at all, it turns out, is necessary. After all, a marriage is a spiritual thing. All they need do is think prayerfully about what they are doing, perhaps read some Scripture, and consider themselves married.

The only difficulty with that sparse and practical approach is that it treats us as though we were disembodied intellects. Our bodies and our imaginations, and indeed our intellects and our hearts, all want to enact the thing. Insofar as we believe, for example, that there is an exquisite mystery called femininity and that virginity itself is a most noble and pure thing, then we want to *bespeak* it all, not just in our thoughts, nor just in propositions and preaching, but with a white and beautiful dress that cries out to heaven, earth, and hell, "Behold! Behold! Here is the bride!" No elaboration is felt to be too rich for the mysteries that lie in just that one small aspect of what is happening at a wedding. The procession itself: why so slow? Is it a dirge? Is the bride reluctant? No. Rather, this stately pace says, "Here is a great and joyous solemnity. Let us not frolic through it." The tempo and the posture *answer to* what we discern to be going on. They give a visible shape to the meaning.

Words alone will not do the trick.

Form and Fabric

All of this touches on the old topic of form and matter: what is the relation between what a thing looks like and what it is? The philosophers have made assaults on the question for centuries, and it seems to lie somehow very near the center of things. In our ordinary experiences we come across it all the time in very workaday situations. An ugly face, for example, seems to be the very diagram of an evil soul, full of lust or egoism or cruelty while another ugly face has somehow been transfigured with the light of charity and radiates beauty. We see a beautiful face from which vanity, petulance, and surfeit glimmer, or a beautiful face aglow with generosity, innocence, and humor. In all of these things, at the back of our sense of how appropriate or how contradictory the relationship seems to be between the surface and what is beneath, there lies the notion that in some perfect realm the outward and the inward are perfectly harmonious. And we are right. Such was the Creation itself, and such will be the redeemed Creation. Meanwhile we can only live with the ambiguities and apparent discrepancies, conscious that the division between the outward and the inward is a division which we brought upon ourselves at the Fall.

In the liturgy of the Church we approach that perfect harmony between the outward and the inward. We celebrate Redemption, which has begun to knit things back together. We anticipate the final Redemption of all things when that restoration will be completed. We recall the Incarnation, in which we find the perfect uniting of form and matter, that is, of perfect wholeness and purity with human flesh. We see in the Second Adam the perfection that was to have been exhibited in the first.

The ceremonies of the liturgy answer to all of this. For in the liturgy we step into redemption, in faith, and bespeak the perfect uniting of the outer and the inner that will be unfurled in the new heavens and the new earth. We renounce the divided world where body wars against heart and where gesture struggles with thought. By enacting what is true, we learn what is true. By bowing with our heads as well as our hearts, we testify to the restored seamlessness of outer and inner. By bowing with the knee we teach our reluctant hearts to bow. By making the sign of the cross with our hands we signal to heaven, earth, hell, and to our own innermost beings that we are indeed under this sign—that we are crucified with Christ. No longer do we refuse the outer gesture in the name of the inner faith. Buddhism, Platonism, and Manichaeanism may do so, but Christian faith cries out to be shaped.

By this time we have come very close to the word, nay the reality, that lies at the center of the liturgy, namely, the Sacrament.

7

Table and Altar:
Supper and Sacrament

The word _sacrament_ means pledge, or mystery. It does not
occur in the Bible, any more than do words like Trinity, substitutionary, prelapsarian, or inerrancy. Christian vocabulary is
full of words that have come into use as the Christian mind has
gone to work on what it finds in the Scripture.

The Sacrament of Christ's Body and Blood is the great
pledge, given by the Lord to His Church, for as long as history
lasts, of the reunion of form and matter, or spirit and flesh. Put
more directly, it presents to us His death, by which He redeemed the world from sin and death and from the ruin
brought on by the Fall. The "rebuilding," or reunion, of things
from this ruin was inaugurated by God in the Old Testament,
manifested at the Incarnation, and will be completed at the Parousia. It is pledged and kept present to us in the Eucharist
which is both memory and anticipation. It recalls Christ's
body, broken for us, and it looks forward to His glorious re-
appearing. "In remembrance of me...till He come."[20] Both
phrases are necessary.

More Than a Memory

The "remembrance" that inheres in the Sacrament is more
than mere recollection, however. The English word does not
quite catch the whole of what lies in the word _anamnesis_,
which Christ used when He gave the bread to His disciples as

His Body. The word suggests a remembering that is also a making present. Many Christians limit the significance of the Eucharist to the idea of recalling bread and wine as aids to memory and devotion. They are certainly at least that, but from its earliest days the Church understood this Eucharist to be Sacrament, mystery.

There is no mystery in a mere aid to memory. The Church, as it pondered what the Lord might have meant in the strange formula, "This is my body," attached great weight to what He said. As with the doctrine of the Trinity, what is not spelled out as such either in the Gospels or by Saint Paul was articulated by the Church very early as what is indeed there in the Scripture. The same is true of this doctrine; no single New Testament text spells out the whole rich treasury of Eucharistic faith.

All springs from the Lord's own stark and mysterious words, not only at the Last Supper itself, but those recorded in John 6:

> ...my Father giveth you the true bread from heaven. For the bread of God is he which cometh down from heaven, and giveth life unto the world....I am the living bread which came down from heaven: if any man eat of this bread, he shall live for ever: and the bread that I will give is my flesh, which I will give for the life of the world. The Jews therefore strove among themselves, saying, How can this man give us his flesh to eat? Then Jesus said unto them, Verily, verily, I say unto you, Except ye eat the flesh of the Son of man, and drink his blood, ye have no life in you. Whoso eateth my flesh, and drinketh my blood, hath eternal life; and I will raise him up at the last day. For my flesh is meat indeed, and my blood is drink indeed. He that eateth my flesh, and drinketh my blood, dwelleth in me, and I in him....This is that bread which came down from heaven....[21]

It is possible to draw the sting from these words by spiritualizing them. The Jews who were so maddened by His words would have been placated if He had agreed to do this. In response to their consternation, He only drives the scandal home: "Except ye eat the flesh of the Son of man, and drink his blood, ye have no life in you." The "except ye" here is precisely the same as in the third chapter of John regarding the new birth. Neither the heavenly birth nor the heavenly food is optional. One cannot get around this point in Scripture.

Those who avoid the scandal here by spiritualizing the Lord's words can indeed hold up their end of the discussion if the letter of the text itself is alone consulted. But in so doing they dissociate themselves from the understanding that the Church has brought to these words for two thousand years. We find that the vast testimony of godly teachers, including some who themselves had been taught by the apostles, speaks of the Eucharist in these sacramental terms.

The Witness of History

Ignatius of Antioch, in his epistle to the Smyrnaeans, spoke of "those who hold strange doctrines.... They abstain from eucharist and prayer, because they allow not that the eucharist is the flesh of our Saviour Jesus Christ."[22]

Justin Martyr, who, like Ignatius, was close in time to the apostles, said, "We do not receive these as common bread or common drink. But just as our Saviour Jesus Christ was made flesh through the Word of God and had both flesh and blood for our salvation, so also we have been taught that the food which has been eucharized by the word of prayer from Him is the flesh and blood of the Incarnate Jesus" (*First Apology*, 66,2). Irenaeus, shortly thereafter, put it thus: "...the bread, which is produced from the earth, when it receives the invocation of God, is no longer common bread, but the Eucharist, consisting of two realities, earthly and heavenly" (*Contra Haereticos*, 4, 18, 5).

Athanasius, to whom we are all indebted for defending the

orthodox Faith against Arianism, said, "But when the great and wondrous prayers have been recited, then the bread becomes the body and the cup the blood of our Lord Jesus Christ" (*Sermon to the Baptized*). Likewise, we find the other witnesses to the faith speaking this way: Basil, Gregory of Nyssa, Hilary, Ambrose, Augustine, Chrysostom, and countless others.

Much later on, John Wycliffe said that the change that occurs at the Eucharist "effects the presence of the body of Christ.... Not that the bread is destroyed, but that it *signifies* the body of the Lord there present in the sacrament" (*De Eucharistia*, 100f.).

The Bohemian Reformer John Hus spoke likewise, "The humble priest doth not...say that he is the creator of Christ, but that the Lord Christ by His power and word, through him, causes that which is bread to be His body; not that at that time it began to be His, but that there on the altar begins to be sacramentally in the form of the bread what previously was not there and therein."

The Reformers also used language that acknowledges great mystery here. Luther wrote in his *Small Catechism*, "What is the Sacrament of the Altar? It is the true Body and Blood of Christ, under the bread and wine." Calvin spoke this way of the matter, in his *Short Treatise on the Holy Supper*:

> It is a spiritual mystery which cannot be seen by the eye nor be comprehended by human understanding. Therefore it is represented for us by means of visible signs, according to the need of our weakness. Nevertheless, it is not a naked figure, but one joined to its truth and substance. With good reason then, the bread is called body, because it not only represents, but also presents it.

Many Christians, alarmed by language like this, dismiss Christ's Eucharistic pledge with a quip about His not being a

literal door even though He said, "I am the door," supposing
thereby that they have dispelled the mystery of the Eucharist.
Twenty centuries of Christian testimony carries no weight with
them. It is not uncommon to hear it urged that the Church—
virtually the whole Church—went off the rails while the apostles were still alive and that only a modern remnant has a true
understanding of the Eucharist, which is that it is no mystery
at all but only an aid to memory.

To take this view is possible. Millions of devout Christians
do. And God Himself alone is the keeper of the mystery. How,
precisely, we may speak of bread and wine as Christ's Body
and Blood is as baffling as how we may speak of Jesus as both
man and God, or of His mother as a virgin, or of the Bible as
the Word of God. The matter will not yield itself either to
chemistry or logic. The attempts to reduce Christ's gift of the
Eucharist to something that we can reasonably cope with are
like the attempts made by modernist Christians to reduce outrages like the Resurrection and the Ascension to figures of
speech that convey abstract truths.

The human mind, and perhaps especially the "spiritual"
mind, has a deep-running suspicion of anything that really
does bridge the gulf between spirit and matter. The Sadducees
hated the threat of this very thing which surfaced in Christ's
claims about Himself. The Jews were scandalized when He
said that He would give them His flesh to eat. All transcendentalists, logicians, Buddhists, and Manichaeans hate this sort of
thing. We must keep spirit and matter in two different realms,
they urge. Spirit is material and may not be supposed ever to
come upon matter, even though just this seems to have happened at the Annunciation, with the starkest results.

The Sacramental Center

At the center of the liturgy, then, stands the Sacrament, the
mystery. We have come a step further than mere metaphor by

this time, towards the center of all things. Metaphor, with all of its variations—simile, symbol, sign, and indeed art itself—says, Let X stand for Y. Let this hexagonal road sign mean "stop." Let this death's head mean "poison." Let this pattern of pigment on canvas stand for Aristotle's contemplating the bust of Homer. Let this shaped piece of marble stand for Venus. Let this kiss stand for loving feelings.

The whole business of taking one thing and pressing it into service so that it will suggest another seems to lie close to the center of things.

The eye of faith would see Sacrament as taking up this "natural" tendency and carrying it across the frontier that divides the seen from the unseen (or the form from the meaning). Here, in the Sacrament, we have not merely metaphor, bread and wine *suggesting* something else. We have the very thing that all metaphor strains at. We have metaphor set free, as it were, to be the thing that it bespeaks. Sacrament is metaphor lifted by redemption from the mortal world, locked as that world is into mere "nature." It is set free, as we will all be at the Resurrection, into the undivided world that was created by God to begin with, divided at the Fall and restored in the Incarnation, to be unfurled finally at the Parousia.

In this sense, Sacrament, recalling and presenting the Incarnation itself, is not so much supernatural as quintessentially natural, because it restores to nature its true function of being full of God. "*Pleni sunt coeli et terra gloria tua*," sings the Church, not in a pantheistic hymn that blurs the distinction between Creator and creation but in testimony that indeed heaven and earth are full of His glory. Nature is the God-bearer, so to speak, not the god, nor God and nature merged.

In this sense also, then, what we modern, scientifically minded men commonly refer to as "natural" turns out to be unnatural, since we usually use the term "natural" to refer strictly to the scheme of things that is locked into mortality. Since nothing in the creation was made to be thus locked, it may be said that insofar as things seem to follow a mere cycle of birth, death, and decay, or that abstract "law" governs everything; then the situation is unnatural; some death-blow has been dealt to things. Christians, like Saint Paul, see nature groaning and struggling under its unnatural burden of mortality, waiting to be set free once more into its native liberty.

In the Sacrament, the eye of faith sees the pledge of this glorious redemption of things. In the merely natural world, all bread presents us with a wonderful metaphor. It is a case in point of the seed's falling into the ground and dying so that it might spring to life again, only to be taken, ground, baked, broken, and given for the life of others. All of this is enacted for us in the natural world. In the Sacrament, bread, which is already a metaphor, is taken and raised to a dignity beyond mere metaphor. It now becomes the very mode under which we may feed, not on mere mortal life, as the Jews did on manna, but on undying life. Like the humble body of the virgin which, from being "only" natural, was raised at the Annunciation to the dignity of being the God-bearer, so the humble stuff of bread at the Eucharist is raised to a similar dignity. Both events scandalize our senses. Virgin birth does not occur. Bread is not flesh.

The Sacrament of the Eucharist is, of course, one step away from the Incarnation itself, where the thing signified (The Word) and the signifier (Jesus) were absolutely one. Symbol and sign and metaphor strain towards this union; Sacrament presents it, but the Incarnation *is* that perfect union. Again, it is a scandal. God is not man, any more than bread is flesh. But faith overrides the implacable prudence of logic and chemistry and says, "Lo!"

Two fragments of hymnody may take all of this complexity and place it somewhat closer to our grasp, if we may speak at all of "grasping" a mystery. The first is a small quatrain, attributed often to Queen Elizabeth I, that gives faith's testimony as it approaches the Eucharist:

His was the word that spake it,
He took the bread and brake it;
And what his word did make it,
That I believe and take it.

The second, and older, fragment, is from Saint Thomas
Aquinas's magisterial Eucharistic hymn, *Pange Lingua*:

Word-made-flesh, true bread he maketh
  By his word his Flesh to be,
Wine his Blood; when man partaketh,
  Though his senses fail to see,
Faith alone, when sight forsaketh,
  Shows true hearts the mystery.

Therefore we, before him bending,
  This great Sacrament revere;
Types and shadows have their ending,
  For the newer rite is here;
Faith, our outward sense befriending,
  Makes our inward vision clear.[23]

Christians who distrust Saint Thomas's supernally high view
of the Sacrament as veering perhaps too close to magic will
note his stress on faith as the key. This mystery, like all of the
gospel mysteries, may be held only by faith, even though it,
like the Incarnation, Resurrection, and Ascension, exists quite
apart from faith, "out there" in the real world.

A Rich Simplicity

When we begin to reflect on things in this manner, we may
begin to see that the apparent distance between the simplicity
of the Last Supper and the complexity of the liturgy—even of
High Mass—is only an illusion.

How can this be?

In the simple act of taking bread, and of blessing, breaking, and giving it to His disciples, the Lord gathered up all the mystery of the gospel: that the Word must become flesh, and that this flesh must be broken for the life of the world, and that unless and until we, His followers, participate in this mystery we have no life in us. Nothing less than this is intimated at the Last Supper, and nothing more than this is celebrated in the liturgy.

At that supper table with His friends, Jesus revealed Himself for what John the Baptist had hailed Him as long before: the Lamb of God which taketh away the sin of the world. Here is My body. Here is My blood. This is the whole Old Testament now brought to its fulfillment. And you, My friends, are invited, not only to be spectators or merely to *recall* what I am doing. You are invited, at this table, to participate in the mystery. When you feed on something, it becomes your very substance. I am uniting you with My own self-offering here.

Suddenly the language of table and altar, so often the occasion for a quarrel, becomes rich with the mystery of the divine charity. Far from being matter for debate and division, it spreads before us the amplitude of Redemption. The altar, the place of holocaust, has become the place of feasting. But the food of this feast is the broken bread and the shed blood. To say that the altar has been merely "replaced" by the table is to stand at one remove from the mystery of the gospel. To say that it has *become* the table, or better, united with the table and fulfilled in it, is to step somewhat closer to what must always remain impenetrable to our mortal understanding. For this reason, Christian piety has given the name *sacrament*—mystery—to what the Lord inaugurated in the upper room.

8

The Eucharistic Liturgy: Diagram and Drama

The Eucharistic liturgy as it was celebrated at The Church of St. Mary the Virgin would have appeared elaborate to a first-time visitor. Many things seemed to be going on. Clearly, much more than a meeting was occurring.

For example, right at the beginning came a solemn procession, with cross, candles (or "lights" as they are called in this tradition), incense (or, rather, a censer, or thurible, full of coals but not yet smoking with the grains of incense, which would be sprinkled on the coals presently), acolytes, and finally the clergy in richly brocaded vestments. During the next ninety minutes or so, there was endless moving about, all with the greatest solemnity and the greatest austerity, and all of it, clearly, carried on in obedience to some overarching set of directions, the way a symphony or ballet must proceed in rigorous obedience to the score or the choreography. A newcomer, even a very devout Christian believer, unfamiliar with these things, might have been inclined to put it all down to elaboration for its own sake.

What this newcomer would presently have discovered, if he had returned often enough, would have been that, far from this ceremony's being an elaboration, it was, rather, an unfurling, or a clarifying. It presented an exact, visible diagram of the whole gospel, accessible to literate and illiterate alike. No gesture was superfluous. Nothing was done for the sake of mere

115

vain show. Nothing was mumbo-jumbo. It was pompous, to be sure, but not in the miserable modern sense of that word. Rather, here was pomp in its earlier, richer sense of high ceremonial things' being done obediently.

There is a curious sense in which it may be said that the more elaborate the celebration of the liturgy, the simpler it is, since in a high mass everything is visible. Nothing is implicit. The diagram is complete. The peasant and the philosopher, and all of us in between, may encounter as much of the gospel as our capacities can sustain, since the whole drama is there.

On the other hand, a high mass has no meaning and no validity other than what is also present in a crust of brown bread, a paper cup of cheap wine, and a few Christians gathered in a hovel or on a beach to remember the Lord's death. We may recall that the hood of a jeep has often furnished the table for men about to go into battle, and we may be sure that the Host who invites us mortals to His table will feed us with the same food whether the surface is tin, linoleum, or marble.

Historic Worship

The liturgy takes somewhat different forms in the various ancient traditions in Christendom, so that a Western Christian, for example, might find himself bewildered at first in a Syrian, Armenian, or Russian church; but he would recognize before very long the familiar "shape of the liturgy," as it is called. For no matter how the liturgy may differ in details, language, or ceremony, from tradition to tradition in the Church, it always enacts and proclaims certain unvarying elements.

The liturgy always begins with the *synaxis*, which simply means the "coming together" of the people, and it always moves to the Great Thanksgiving, or Communion.

The synaxis is usually called "the liturgy of the Word," for in this first part of the Christian liturgy the Scripture is read and preached. In most traditions there will be readings from the Old Testament, the Epistles, and the Gospels, with the Psalms also used at certain points. This part of the liturgy includes the sermon, or homily, the Creed, and sometimes the intercessory prayers. In the early Church, outsiders were permitted to come to the synaxis so that they might hear the Scripture read and preached and possibly be converted. Also, the "catechumens," that is, new believers who were being prepared for baptism over several months of instruction, were present at the synaxis.

When the Church came to the Great Thanksgiving, all outsiders, and all unbaptized believers were sent out. Now the Church came to its holiest mysteries, and only the fully initiated could participate.

This makes it sound cultic to our modern ears, accustomed as we are to the happy gregariousness that wants above all else to fill up the church auditorium. There is a sense in which it was, indeed, and still should be, "cultic," if by this we refer to holy and even in some sense secret mysteries, and not to the heresies and fevered conventicles to which the word *cult* is usually applied now. Even to speak of secret mysteries at all is to conjure for most people a dark picture of obscene grottoes, bacchanalia, saturnalia, and Eleusinian rites.

To be sure, the Christian mysteries share with those depraved rites at least this, that the god really is believed to be present and that what is occurring is incomprehensible to the uninitiated. But the difference between the two is the difference between heaven and hell, between holiness and obscenity, between liberty and bondage, between reality and fraud.

The Sequence of the Liturgy

The following description presents the liturgy as it is widely celebrated in the Western church now. The sequence we see here resembles the sequence that took shape over the first century or two of the Church's life, which one can read about in very ancient descriptions of Christian worship. The account given here includes only the principal sections of the liturgy. Technical manuals explain things in far greater detail.[24]

To see the choir, servers, and clergy entering the church in procession during the singing of a hymn is very common, although strictly speaking the liturgy itself has not yet begun. (The Orthodox church has a somewhat different view on this point.) But the church, that is, the people of God, is gathered now and begins to enact what is true, namely, that the Church here on earth, together with the Church in heaven, moves in its worship to the place of God's dwelling. The procession follows the cross up to the altar, a vivid picture of what is indeed true: the Church does approach God covered by the cross. Everyone in the congregation and all Christians everywhere are "in" the procession as it moves toward the altar, singing with angels and the saints of all ages.

THE GREETING

The celebrant begins the liturgy with the words, "Blessed be God, Father, Son, and Holy Spirit." The people answer, "And blessed be His kingdom, now and for ever. Amen."

This, in a nutshell, is the whole of worship.[25] This is the song of the morning stars at the Creation; it is sung by angels and archangels and all the company of heaven; we mortals were put here on earth to sing it; and we will sing it forever in Paradise. Hell hates this song. Evil cannot sing it at all. For in it is gathered up the joyous order of heaven and earth, namely, that God is to be blessed by His creatures.

This is the very thing that all creatures—all angels, and all men, and all beasts and creeping things, and all floods, thunders, dragons, and great deeps—were made for. To learn to sing this is to begin to approach a joy that is unimaginable to the worldly mind. We see what God is and what He has done, and we, with the whole creation, respond with "Blessed!" Pride and egocentrism see the same thing and abominate it. Here is the difference between heaven and hell. The liturgy unfurls heaven for us. It is a tutor, so to speak, teaching us the vocabulary of heaven.

THE COLLECT

The celebrant then says the Collect for Purity: "Almighty God, unto whom all hearts are open, all desires known, and from whom no secrets are hid: Cleanse the thoughts of our hearts by the inspiration of thy Holy Spirit, that we may perfectly love thee, and worthily magnify thy holy Name; through Christ our Lord. Amen." We want to be enabled to worship God, and pure hearts are required of those who will come into the Divine Presence (see Ps. 24:4; Matt. 5:8). Therefore we ask in this prayer for pure hearts.

THE HYMNS

Then follows an ancient hymn. There are five of these that occur during the course of the liturgy, and it is the musical settings to these that one hears in a mass by Palestrina, Bach, or Mozart, although most congregations sing them to simple tunes or even say them. The first is the *Kyrie*, or, to give it its whole title, the *Kyrie Eleison* (pronounced *kee*-ree-eh ay-*lay*-ee-zawn). This is the Greek for "Lord, have mercy," and if the congregation sings it, it is almost always sung in English.

To the early Christians, "Kyrie!" was an acclamation like a shout of greeting to an emperor and not a penitential cry at all. With the addition of the petition "Have mercy" Christians understood the *Kyrie* as making a request appropriate at the beginning of the liturgy because everyone needs the Lord's mercy to be received by Him and to worship Him. It is fitting because it bespeaks an attitude that is right and healthy for us mortals at all times. We live and move and have our being in God, as indeed the whole Creation does. The whole universe depends on His mercy, and we humans appear to have been assigned the special task of articulating in behalf of all mortal creatures what the rest of them cannot put into words: supplication, thanks, adoration.

Hence, it is right that we have these cries on our lips frequently, but not because, like the pagans, we fear that this God might not have mercy or that we will not be able to get His attention. Christians from nonliturgical traditions sometimes wonder whether this cry does not betray a faulty faith. Has not God already had mercy on us? Why ask for it?

Just as it is appropriate for us to say often to the people we love that we love them, even though it has been true for years, or for us to thank the Lord for His goodness even though we thanked Him yesterday for the same thing, so for our own sakes it is healthy to keep on our lips what is true always and daily, namely, that we owe our well-being to His steadfast mercy. There are many requests like this in the New Testament. "Thy kingdom come," the Lord taught us to pray, even though God's kingdom has come and will come whether we join in the prayer or not. But prayer is at least partly a matter of our placing ourselves in the right postures and attitudes. It does no good to pit doctrines like God's sovereignty (He will do what He will do) against the command that we pray. In a mystery, He wants our prayers. No formula throws a single glint of light on the relationship between whether we pray or how much we pray and what God does.

In festal seasons of the year, instead of the hymn *Kyrie*, the *Gloria* is sung. All Christians are familiar at least with the opening lines of this hymn, since it is what the angels sang at the Nativity: "Glory be to God on high, and on earth peace, good will towards men." The *Gloria* is a hymn of pure worship. It supplies us with words we might have to grope for if we were left to our own resources. There is nothing about our own feelings and experiences in the *Gloria*. Like the *Te Deum*, and like the task of worship itself, its task is to ascribe worth to God, not to express feelings or to share experiences.

Another very brief canticle is sometimes sung here, known as the *Trisagion* ("thrice holy"): "Holy God, Holy and Mighty, Holy Immortal One, Have mercy upon us." It is an exceedingly ancient hymn in the Church.

COLLECT FOR THE DAY

Then follows the Collect for the Day. In one sentence, this prayer makes a request of the Lord, usually in the light of the particular gospel event or idea that the liturgy for that day remembers. For example, on Easter we ask that we might die daily to sin and live in the joy of the Resurrection, or on the Ascension we ask that "we may also in heart and mind thither ascend." This brief prayer strikes the note for the liturgy of that day.

READING OF THE SCRIPTURES

The reading of Scripture follows the Collect for the Day. Such reading has been central to all Christian worship from the start and to Hebrew worship before that. It is necessary to place ourselves under the Word of God. At the end of the reading of the Old Testament lesson, and of the epistle, the people respond with "Thanks be to God."

This is far from being an empty formula. "Thanks be to God" may not be at all what one feels about what he has just heard, which might have included some very jarring words from a prophet, or a demanding bit of teaching from Saint Paul. One might be much more inclined to murmur, "Not for me," or "Much too severe."

But the liturgy teaches us to say, "Thanks be to God," for if we could see all things clearly, we would see that the Word of God, even in its most frightening and taxing aspects, is liberating and life-giving to us. It points the way to fullness and joy for us; so that even where it jolts us, it is our very health.

Once again, the liturgy "imposes" on us the right thing to say; thus helping us along our way to the place where the external rules and the internal responses of our hearts coincide. Such a state of affairs is called sanctity, and it is synonymous with freedom; the righteousness anticipated by the Law, and given to us in Christ, has now become a living reality in the inner man. The liturgy is a tutor in this school.

The reading from the Gospel is the high point of this part of the liturgy. The Old Testament reading has anticipated it, and the Epistle has commented on it; but in the Gospel itself we have the Lord's own life and words. In many churches the Gospel reading occurs from a point in the aisle, with the people surrounding it and facing it, enacting the idea of the Lord's speaking His words to His gathered people from their very midst. The people respond to the reading with "Praise be to thee, O Christ."

THE PREACHING OF THE GOSPEL

After the Gospel is read, the Word is preached. Since liturgical worship is a whole and single act rather than a collage, we do not need to hunt for special items in it that qualify as "worship" as opposed to other items that are peripheral. The preaching of the Word is not a pause or a diversion in the liturgy, even though it may take the form of instruction, reproof, warning, or consolation. Faithful preaching will always take the people along the way towards the altar of God, as it were. It is part of the mystery of the Church that to her has been given the task of guarding and teaching the Word of God. According to the New Testament, not everyone in the Church has authority to teach officially, and no one at all has a warrant to bring private interpretations to the Scriptures. This is what spawns heresies, and it is against the clutter of private interpretations that the teaching office of the Church stands.

The people respond to the preaching of the Word by standing and confessing together the Faith to which this preaching has turned their attention. The ancient Nicene Creed is used here. It spells out in detail what Christians believe to be the irreducible core of the gospel. It is not a mere doctrinal outline; it is a confession, not in the sense of penitence for sin but in the sense of a glad telling out of what the Church believes. The "facts," or mysteries, that we list in the Creed are what rouse adoration in our hearts and songs from our lips.

INTERCESSORY PRAYER

The Prayer of Intercession, or as it is sometimes called, the Prayers of the People, follows the creed. The Bible teaches that Christ is in heaven as our high priest, offering intercession for us. But His is not a solitary priesthood; He has made His Church a part of it. Saint Peter teaches that we are a royal priesthood. Priests make offering, and part of the offering which the Church shares with her High Priest is the offering of intercessions.

In prayer, as with the Sacraments themselves, we find ourselves on the frontier between time and eternity. Logically it does not make sense; God's will is going to be done whether we ask for things or not, or so it would appear. It seems nonsense to think of our changing either God's mind or the crushing onward movement of history, especially when we pray for general things like peace in the Middle East or for starving millions somewhere. If our religious training has taught us that praying is mainly a matter of our making specific, private, "answerable" requests, we may have some difficulty with these sweeping and general public intercessions.

We may recall, however, in this connection, that the mystery of prayer goes back to the beginning of things and that we have been commanded to pray. No doubt, only eternity will reveal the connection between the march of history and the continual offering of intercessions by the people of God. Meanwhile, the liturgy obliges us to enter into the ministry of intercession, which our High Priest offers at the Throne.

The one item among the Prayers of the People that might arouse more questions than others, at least among Christians unaccustomed to the practice, is the prayers for the dead.

The hesitancy about prayers for the dead generally runs something like this: the dead are certainly beyond our reach, and their fate is now in God's hands. It is inappropriate to pray for them, since their story is finished.

The reply might run like this: which of our requests, big or small, does not touch something beyond our reach? And where else but in God's hands is the fate of anyone, living or dead?

The notion that a man's whole story is finished at the precise point of physical death and his destiny fixed and sealed is not made clear in the Bible. The text, "...it is appointed unto man once to die, but after this the judgment," in Hebrews 9:27, which is often advanced in discussions on this point, tells us nothing more than what is obvious: we die once, and then begins the whole business of "judgment," whatever that may entail for every soul. The Bible does not vouchsafe us much light on how, much less when, our stories reach completion in the realm beyond death.

What the Church prays for in its prayers for the dead is twofold. First, it prays for the believing dead, that the work of grace begun in them in this life will go on until they reach "the measure of the stature of the fullness of Christ."[26] The Bible does not oblige us to think either that this work of grace halts in its tracks when physical death occurs or that it is suddenly rushed to miraculous completion.

Once more, we must not confuse time with eternity. How that process of glorification is completed we cannot imagine, but neither our pictures of "one instant" or of "aeons" tell the story quite adequately, any more than our notions about obstetrics tell the story of the Virgin birth. Presumably Abel, the first man to die, will not have been dead any "longer" than the man who dies an instant before the last trump. So we pray for the believing dead, trusting that because of Jesus' Resurrection we have one unbroken fellowship with them. We deny death as an ultimate barrier.

Second, the Church prays for all the dead. This is more difficult, since it looks as though they might have gone completely beyond the pale of prayer if they have not been part of the fellowship of the Church. But they are still part of the huge fabric of Creation, and nothing in that fabric is beyond the scope of mercy. We cannot tell God what to do with them or speak with any certainty of what He is at any given point doing with them, but we can commend them to the mystery of His mercy, as we commend all things thus. We must not be too hasty or fierce or cavalier in reaching conclusions about the judgment that Scripture spells out. God is the judge; we are priests, part of whose ministry is to offer prayer for all people.

CONFESSION OF SIN

At the end of the Intercessions, it is not uncommon to find the Confession of Sin. All Christians are familiar with the practice of private confession, in which we bare our hearts to God. In the public, general act of confession in the liturgy, we place ourselves in a right attitude by saying what is true, namely, that we have in fact sinned in thought, word, and deed, and that we need God's forgiveness. Left to our private feelings and resources, we might gradually drift from this stark awareness. Here again the liturgy is our teacher, giving us the words to say and thus assisting us to enter rightly into the corporate worship of the Church.

The priest does not himself forgive our sins; He declares God's forgiveness on the basis of Christ's merits alone. The priest is not a mediator whom the Church has interposed between Christ and us. Rather, his is the voice we hear, declaring that it is God who forgives sins. Because we are flesh and blood creatures and not pure intellects, it is a great help to us to hear these words, audibly and coming from outside ourselves altogether. In the absolution, as in the entire liturgy, we are lifted away from the tangle of our private efforts to believe and grasp these great things. We find ourselves in the realm where they are declared to be true, no matter how feeble our own faith or how despondent our feelings may be.

THE KISS OF PEACE

The peace now follows. It is perhaps one of the most ancient exchanges of all in the liturgy. Here we offer each other "the peace of the Lord." As with the opening acclamation of the liturgy, so here, we the Church are the visible, audible, flesh-and-blood sign and herald and presence on earth of the kingdom of heaven whose citizens always fervently and joyfully offer each other this peace.

Once again, hell hates this, and sin does its best to destroy it; but in the liturgy we proclaim and enact it and resolve that it will be proclaimed and enacted in our attitudes and acts during the rest of the week. Quite appropriately, we are asked by the liturgy to exchange this greeting, this kiss of peace, with whoever happens to be near us at the moment: spouses, siblings, parents, friends, strangers, and even people who irritate us, perhaps even our enemies. We do not have the luxury of picking and choosing the ones we might prefer to greet thus. Charity greets everyone indiscriminately with this greeting. The liturgy gives us an elementary lesson in charity: "Salute one another with an holy kiss."[27]

The exchange of peace brings the synaxis to an end. Now the Church moves into the Great Thanksgiving, or the Communion. The first act here is the Offertory.

THE OFFERTORY

The liturgy does not huddle the collection of money into a sort of parenthesis called "Announcements and Offering." Since the entire action of the liturgy is an offering of thanks, of adoration, of ourselves, and of our substance, all taken up into the one perfect offering, and thus made acceptable—since this is so, everything that we bring is hallowed. Indeed, the gathering and offering of money is part of the same movement in which the bread and wine are brought from the back of the church to the altar, since all of it represents the common stuff of our lives, the firstfruits and substance of our work and of ourselves.

Bread and wine are universal symbols representing the common stuff of human life. In the liturgy, as in Redemption, that common stuff is taken and "transubstantiated," if we will, and given back to us by God as the food of eternal life. He does this with whatever we will offer to Him. Suffering itself, a purely negative thing from a worldly point of view, can be thus transubstantiated and become glorious, if it is made into an offering. We glimpse at this mystery in the Offertory.

In response to the Offertory, the two ancient hymns *Sanctus* and *Benedictus* are sung. In the Preface to these, the celebrant says the following words: "It is very meet, right, and our bounden duty, that we should at all times, and in all places, give thanks unto thee, O Lord, holy Father, almighty, everlasting God." Then, after a "Proper Preface," which links this acclamation with the special focus of that day's liturgy, he continues: "Therefore with Angels and Archangels, and with all the company of heaven, we laud and magnify thy glorious Name; evermore praising Thee, and saying," whereupon the people join with, "Holy, holy, holy, Lord God of Hosts. Heaven and earth are full of thy glory. Glory be to thee, O Lord most high. Blessed is he that cometh in the name of the Lord. Hosanna in the highest."

In the words "Therefore with Angels and Archangels" we find articulated especially clearly the notion, already touched upon in these pages, that in its worship the Church finds the veil between earth and heaven drawn aside. In the greeting "Hosanna!" we greet Him who came to Jerusalem on a humble donkey and who now comes to us in the humble forms of bread and wine.

THE EUCHARISTIC PRAYER

The great Eucharistic Prayer now follows. In most forms of this prayer, we find a rehearsal of God's mighty acts in Creation and Redemption, leading up to the words "This is my Body....This is my Blood." It seems to have been the pattern for this prayer, established early in the Church and followed everywhere since.

Other major elements in this prayer have been the *Unde et memores* and the *Epiclesis*. In the *Unde et memores* we declare to God that what we are doing we do in obedience to Christ's institution and in remembrance of His Passion and Resurrection. In some form of the *Epiclesis*, or "calling down upon," we beseech the Holy Ghost to come upon us and upon the bread and wine, so that what is intended by the liturgy will indeed, in very truth, occur, since without the Holy Ghost the liturgy is a charade.

At the end of the Eucharistic Prayer, the Lord's Prayer is said, and then the celebrant breaks the Bread, in full view of all the people, saying, "Christ our Passover is sacrificed for us." The people respond with, "Therefore let us keep the feast."

THE COMMUNION

One of the great fears expressed by Western Christians who broke from the Eucharistic tradition of the Church in the sixteenth century was that the language of the liturgy seemed to imply that Christ's sacrifice, which had manifestly occurred once in history, was being repeated every time Mass was said. But the arguments on both sides of this question have too often ignored the sense in which the liturgy, like prayer itself, pierces through mere time and, in the mystery of *anamnesis*, "makes present" that which has indeed occurred only once, and once and for all.

No human formulary can quite satisfy us here. Christ died once, but his broken body and poured out blood are given to us now in the Eucharist. His sacrifice, made from the foundation of the world, was brought about in our history under Pontius Pilate and is always present in the heavenly temple, as it is in the Eucharist here on earth. This has been the Church's faith since the beginning.

The hymn *Agnus Dei*, "O Lamb of God, that takest away the sins of the world, have mercy upon us...grant us thy peace," may be sung just before the people receive the bread and wine. After that, the liturgy ends very simply with a prayer of thanksgiving and usually, then, with the blessing and dismissal: "Go in peace to love and serve the Lord," says the deacon.

"Thanks be to God," we respond.

THE DISMISSAL

The dismissal is immensely significant. Whereas the central mysteries of other religions have beckoned the faithful farther and farther into the murk of the shrine, away from the plain light of humdrum human daily life, the Christian mysteries, dark and impenetrable as they are, land us immediately back in that plain light. What we have celebrated at the altar is not only meaningless, but a sacrilege, if it is not carried thence and made present to others under the species of our flesh and blood. It has been the Divine Charity presiding at this altar, and that was the Charity that gave Himself for the life of the world. Insofar as we claim access to that charity at all in the Eucharist, we ourselves become vessels to bear It to a hungry world, as the bread and wine have brought life to us. What are we but the Body of Christ?

"Thanks be to God!" we say, which is to say, "Eucharist!" Even this phrase is freighted with meaning. The Christian life is not drudgery. Like Christ's life, which was an unceasing eucharist, so this life offers its thanks to God unceasingly, even while it is being broken for the life of the world.

9

The Liturgical Year: Redeeming the Time

All Christians from all traditions are familiar with the way in which the truths of the gospel must be transposed into the sequence under which we mortals live, namely, time.

The Resurrection for example, occurred once in history. We embrace this, and we live in the light of it, and Saint Paul teaches us that it is only insofar as this external event becomes a living, daily, inner principle for us that we can be said to have any new life at all. "I am crucified with Christ," Paul wrote, "nevertheless I live; If ye then be risen with Christ...; walk in newness of life."[28] All Christians are familiar with this teaching, and the theme formed the central motif of all evangelical teaching on the "deeper life" as I was growing up.

This truth, which is both a once-for-all event in history and a daily inner principle, also finds itself marked perpetually in the sequence of passing time. "The Lord's Day" is the weekly feast of the Resurrection, in all of Christendom, even in those sectors that disavow all observance of days. This one exception must be made by these Christians, since the New Testament makes it clear that the day was thus kept.

Time and Mystery

There is a profound mystery at work here, touching on the threefold sense in which the gospel is true for Christian believers. Everything recorded in the Gospels happened once in actual history; but these events must be translated by the Holy Ghost into the Christian's own life (Christ must be born in us; we must be circumcised in the inner man; we must be crucified with Him and raised with Him and ascend with Him); and, thirdly, we must perpetually keep coming back in our minds to these events, marking and remembering them, and meditating on them.

We mortals live by hours, days, and weeks, so this marking and remembering must take on some actual, temporal form for us, whether that means we put our minds to these topics whenever the whim takes us or when our routine Bible reading brings us across them, or according to some system which brings us around to them regularly. It is not enough to suppose that having assented once upon a time to a doctrine is sufficient. Every Christian knows that this lofty estimate of our own powers far overshoots the reality of actual life. We need to keep coming back around and putting our minds to the Nativity, the Resurrection, and so forth.

All Christian churches at least theoretically acknowledge that the "Sunday worship service" is a commemoration of the Resurrection, although the notion is somewhat blurred in evangelicalism where worship has taken on a generalized aspect. The liturgical churches, on the other hand, explicitly and avowedly celebrate the Resurrection weekly. Almost the whole Church, furthermore, carries this one step further and agrees that it is not a bad thing to remember two great gospel events, the Nativity and the Resurrection, in a special way once each year. No one knows much about the actual dates in the calendar year when Christ was born and when He rose, but few make an issue of it. The point for all Christians is that on such and such a day the Church marks and celebrates these great events of our salvation.

The Christian Year

This is the principle underlying the so-called Christian year, or liturgical year. More than two events occurred in the gospel drama, says the ancient Church. There is a whole sequence of mysterious and marvelous events that the Lord passed through in His life here on earth, each one of which is most glorious in its significance and most salutary for us to think on.

Hence, the liturgical year is nothing more (and nothing less) than the Church's "walking through" the gospel with the Lord. Since it is a plain fact of our humanness that we are rhythmic creatures who must keep coming back to things that are always true, it is especially good for us to do this in the Church. We do it in our natural lives: someone is born and is with us, day after day, year after year, but once a year we mark this ever-present fact. We marry and take up daily life with spouses year after year, but once a year we find that it is a good thing to mark this ever-present fact, not because it is less true on other days but because we are the sort of creature that is helped and filled with joy when the routines and ever-present facts are set apart, gilded, and held up for our contemplation and celebration.

Somehow the rhythmic, ceremonial return to the ever-present fact helps us. It enriches our apprehension of the thing; whereas, left to our own capacity to keep things alive in our minds, we might find that they have sunk into a kind of autumnal dimness. They need to be revivified, not because *they* dwindle in significance between times, but because *we* dwindle in our capacity to stay alive to them.

There would lie the natural principle behind the liturgical year. Saint Paul forbids two things, however. First, we are not allowed to quarrel with fellow-Christians about the topic, since consciences differ and to one man setting a day aside looks like paganism whereas to another it is a great help. Second, we must not be legalistic or superstitious about observance. The commemorated day itself is not magic. Keeping Easter is not going to raise us with Christ, and missing the day is not going to rob us of the fruits of His Resurrection.

The whole calendar of gospel events was observed with the

greatest amplitude and joy at The Church of St. Mary the Virgin. Feast after feast came and went during the course of a year, and one felt that one was walking very close to this great drama of Redemption. There was a perpetual sense of joy and anticipation, as though to say, "Now we are coming to Advent!" or "Now comes the Transfiguration!"

ADVENT

The liturgical year begins with the season of Advent, which comprises the four Sundays leading up to Christmas. The word *advent* means simply "a coming to," and in the case of the Church year it refers to both of Christ's comings to us, in His humility at His birth and in His glory at the end of time. Hence, it is a season of penitence and self-examination. This strikes newcomers as odd. Here we are approaching *Christmas* and this is a penitential season? How bleak.

A small pause will open to us something infinitely more profound than the tingle of joy we feel when we anticipate Christmas with all of its merrymaking. The Lord is coming! Who of us will not want to be granted some time to make his heart ready? Who of us will deny that this making ready will involve the most earnest self-examination? Raise the significance of the whole thing by including the final coming of Christ as judge at the trump of doom, and it becomes apparent why the Church has designated Advent as a season of self-examination and penitence.

To me as an evangelical the word *penitence* struck a false note at first. I visualized flagellantes and *penitencios* trudging through the streets of Madrid all hooded and chained and carrying crosses, in dread efforts to expiate their sins. I had always wanted to hail them with "There is therefore now no condemnation to them which are in Christ Jesus!"[29] But that darkness and fear is not the note struck by the word *penitence* in this context. Rather, Christians are encouraged to give sober thought to their lives, probing heart and motives, words and actions, attitudes and habits, in the spirit of Saint Paul's injunctions in Romans 13:11-12: "...now it is high time to awake out of sleep: for now is our salvation nearer than when we believed. The night is far spent, the day is at hand: let us therefore cast off the works of darkness, and let us put on the armour of light."

To a Christian unfamiliar with this sort of thing, the whole of Advent might look like a charade. The Lord is not coming on December 25, it might be objected, any more than He is coming one minute from now. Isn't this merely play-acting?

Once more, the answer is to be found in the profoundest mysteries of our humanness. Of course the Lord is here. Of course one needs to keep moment-by-moment account of one's heart, so to speak. But as we have seen in the case of birth, marriage, and death, somehow ceremonializing what is true does have the effect of assisting us. We are not seraphim, who, we are told, can gaze unblinkingly at reality all the time. We have to come at it by fits and starts. To enact something by an act of will does turn out to have its effect in our hearts. If the principle were false, then the early Christians would have been mistaken to have gathered on Sundays to mark the Resurrection. Somehow the weekly ceremony brought home to them what they believed hourly and daily.

The days of Advent are almost inexpressibly powerful. Some of the best hymns of the Christian year occur then. "Come, Thou Long-Expected Jesus" and "O Come, O Come, Emmanuel" place us in imagination alongside all those who for so many centuries waited in the dimness for this great light. "On Jordan's banks the Baptist's cry/Announces that the Lord is nigh"—what thrill of anticipation fills this hymn. My own favorite, I believe, is "Hark, a thrilling voice is sounding,/Christ is nigh it seems to say."

The intensity of joy borne in these hymns is unimaginable to one who has never moved through this season. One cannot omit "Lo, He Comes with Clouds Descending," with its overwhelming evocation of "Those dear tokens of his passion/Still his dazzling body bears...Thousand, thousand saints attending/Swell the triumph of his train:/Alleluia!"

The Nativity makes all good Christian men rejoice. Here again, there is a hymnology that far exceeds the bounds of the half-dozen popular carols to which much American Christianity has confined itself, although the mystery of this birth is caught exquisitely, to be sure, in the familiar words of *Adeste, Fideles*, and "How silently, how silently,/The wondrous gift is given!/...No ear may hear His coming...O Come to us, abide with us,/Our Lord Emmanuel!" The ancient Nativity hymn "Of the Father's Love Begotten" takes us all the way to the cavernous mysteries of heaven where the Trinity dwells surrounded by the celestial hosts.

THE DAYS OF CHRISTMAS

The Feast of the Holy Innocents follows immediately, and ironically, on the heels of Christmas, on December 28. The Church is not delicate about these things, and insofar as this horror stemmed from the Nativity we had better put our minds to what it all might mean. Why should we recall this slaughter and the bloody Herod? Because, says the Church, here as at the cross, we find the point at which the joy of heaven and the evil of hell meet on our earth. Innocent babes killed by the score just when the Savior arrives? What sort of a drama is this? We are driven beyond the sentimentalism that wishes to hear nothing at all but the jingling of bells to the sense in which the flesh of this new infant will itself gather up all the suffering and evil ever perpetrated and will bear it all right on through to Good Friday, Holy Saturday, Easter, and the Ascension.

January 1 is not primarily New Year's Day for the Church. Rather, it is the Feast of the Circumcision, or, as it is often called, of the Holy Name, since it was technically at circumcision that a Jewish child received his name. Certainly, at least two things present themselves for our contemplation on this feast. First, here is the first wound received by the pure flesh of the incarnate God in His identification with us under the Law. And second, here is the name of Jesus. It is the holy name. In it lies our salvation.

In my own evangelical tradition we were taught to love Jesus. We invited Jesus into our hearts. We had His name on our lips all the time. We pressed it on unbelievers, asking them to accept it. We knew Him, we said. We were fervently devoted to Jesus, and rightly so.

But never once in my life had I thought of "The Holy Name," much less of any great feast day of the Church in which we might all ponder the mystery of that name. Now I encountered it in the rhythm of the Church year, as a discipline, and my vision was enlarged. A fifteenth-century Latin hymn, appropriate for this day, expresses what we might want to say:

> To the Name of our salvation
> Laud and honor let us pay,
> Which for many a generation
> Hid in God's foreknowledge lay;
> But with holy exultation
> We may sing aloud today.
> Therefore we, in love adoring,
> This most blessed Name revere,
> Holy Jesus, Thee imploring
> So to write it in us here
> That hereafter, heavenward soaring,
> We may sing with angels there.[30]

The collect in the Roman Missal for this day puts the matter simply: "Lord, You have appointed Your only-begotten Son to be the Saviour of mankind and given Him the name of Jesus;

grant in Your goodness that we who venerate His holy Name on earth may also enjoy the sight of Him in heaven."[31]

EPIPHANY

The Holy Name is followed by the Epiphany on January 6, which recalls the visit of the magi. In the church of my childhood we had always put the camels and the kings right in the manger scene with the shepherds, although we knew that the two groups hadn't arrived all at once. But the Epiphany carries great joy for all believers who are not Jews, and the Orthodox church celebrates this day with more festivity than it does Christmas, since the Epiphany represents the manifestation of Christ to the Gentiles.

All of Saint Paul's preaching about our being "grafted" into the tree comes rushing in. The whole Old Testament suddenly opens up for us all. That which was hidden in the tiny tribe of Israel suddenly floods the world. This Jewish infant is manifest as the *world's* salvation! A great hymn catches this joy:

> Songs of thankfulness and praise,
> Jesus, Lord, to Thee we raise,
> Manifested by the star
> To the sages from afar;
> Branch of royal David's stem
> In Thy birth at Bethlehem;
> Anthems be to Thee addrest
> God in man made manifest.[32]

The Anglican collect for this day reads thus: "O God, who by the leading of a star didst manifest thy only-begotten Son to the Gentiles; Mercifully grant that we, who know thee now by faith, may after this life have the fruition of thy glorious Godhead."

THE PRESENTATION OF CHRIST

After the Epiphany comes the Presentation of Christ in the temple, on February 2. This feast day is sometimes called the

Purification of the Blessed Virgin, and sometimes Candlemas. At this feast we are brought to ponder what it all might mean that the Son of God must tread through all the steps required by the Law. The feast is crowned with Simeon's hymn, "Lord, now lettest thou thy servant depart in peace."

What is the nature of that purity of heart that was able to see salvation in this child; whereas, the Pharisees, looking at the same child presently, could see only threat and imposture? The candles lighted on this day represent the entrance of Christ, the true Light, into the temple.

The fifth collect in the Roman Missal for this day makes the following petition:

> Lord Jesus Christ, who appeared this day among men in the substance of our flesh, presented in the temple by Your parents whom the venerable old man Simeon, enlightened by the rays of Your Spirit, recognized and received and blessed, mercifully grant that we, enlightened and taught by the grace of the same Holy Spirit, may truly acknowledge You and faithfully love You, who live and reign world without end.

GREAT LENT AND HOLY WEEK

Presently Lent arrives. This is the forty days leading up to Easter, which also recall the forty days of Christ's temptation in the wilderness. There is a telescoping of things here, since His temptation did not in actual fact immediately precede His Passion, but "liturgical time" is such that spiritual significance may override chronological exactness.

Lent, like Advent, is a time of penitence. Here we identify ourselves with the Lord's fast and ordeal in the wilderness, which He bore for us.

This raises a point worth noting in passing. There are some varieties of Protestant theology and spirituality that so stress "the finished work of Christ" and the fact that He accomplished everything, that they leave no room at all for any participation on our part. Such participation, encouraged by the ancient Church, does not mean that we mortals claim any of the merit that attaches to Christ's work, much less that we can by one thousandth particle add to His work. Nevertheless, the gospel teaches us that Christians are more than mere followers of Christ. We are His Body and are drawn, somehow, into His own sufferings. We are even "crucified" with Him.

My own tradition stressed this, but it was taught as a metaphor that meant only the putting to death of sin in our members. There was very little said about the sense in which Christ draws His Body into His very self-giving for the life of the world and makes them part of this mystery. Saint Paul uses extravagant language about his own filling up "that which is behind of the afflictions of Christ."[33] We had succinct enough explanations as to what he might have meant here, but these explanations allowed no room for any notion of our participating in Christ's offering. This was looked upon as heresy, violating the doctrine of grace in which all is done by God and nothing by us. We are recipients only. That the gracious donation of salvation by God could in any manner include His making us a part of it all, as He made the Virgin Mary an actual part of the process, and as Saint Paul seems to teach, was not the note struck.

The ancient Church, in its observance of Lent, once more asks us to move through the gospel with Christ Himself. The most obvious mark of Lent to a newcomer is the matter of fasting. I had known about this practice all my life. My Catholic playmates would give up chocolates or Coke or ice cream for Lent. I also knew that a few devout people in my own tradition of evangelicalism practiced fasting now and again for special purposes—a time of especially concentrated prayer, for example.

I myself thought of Lenten fasting and also of the old Catholic practice of refusing meat on Fridays as being legalistic, and perhaps even heretical, since it seemed to entail some notion of accruing merit. Since Christ had done all, why should we flagellate ourselves this way? Was it not a return to the weak and beggarly elements condemned by Saint Paul? Was it not to be guilty of the very thing that the apostle had assailed the Galatian Christians for?

I discovered that the ancient Church teaches just what the New Testament teaches on the point, namely, that fasting is a salutary thing for us to undertake. Jesus fasted and assumed that His followers would. *"When* ye fast,"[34] He said, not "if." Saint Paul both practiced it and taught it. It seems to constitute a reminder to us that our appetites are not all and that man shall not live by bread alone. Furthermore, if we may believe the universal testimony of Christians who do practice it, it also clarifies our spiritual vision somehow. Lastly, it is a token of the Christian's renunciation of the world. There is no *thing* that a Christian will insist he must have at all costs. Fasting supplies an elementary lesson here.

Lent asks us to ponder Christ's self-denial for us in the wilderness. It draws us near to the mystery of Christ's bearing temptation for us in His flesh, and of how in this Second Adam our flesh, which failed in Adam, now triumphs.

Lent also leads us slowly toward that most holy and dread of all events, the Passion of Christ. What Christian will want to arrive at Holy Week with his heart unexamined, full of foolishness, levity, and egoism? To those for whom any special observances hint of legalism or superstition one can only bear witness that the solemn sequence of Lent turns out to be something very different from one's private attempts at meditating on the Passion. To move through the disciplines in company with millions and millions of other believers all over the world is a profoundly instructive thing.

Lent begins with Ash Wednesday. The first time ashes were imposed on my forehead, I found a cacophony of voices inside me: "Come! Now you have betrayed your background! This is straight back to the Dark Ages. Fancy Saint Paul's doing this!"

I knew it was not so when the priest came along with the little pot of damp ashes and with his thumb smudged my forehead—*my forehead*, the very frontal and crown of my dignity as a human being!—and said, "Remember, O man, that dust thou art and unto dust thou shalt return."

I knew it was true. I would return to dust, like all men, but never before had mortality come home to me in this way. Oh, I had believed it spiritually. But surely we need not dramatize it this way....

Perhaps we should, says the Church. Perhaps it is good for our souls' health to recall that our salvation, far from papering over the grave, leads us through it and raises our very mortality to glory. We, like all men, must die. I felt the strongest inclination to wave the priest past as he approached me in the line of people kneeling at the rail. Not me—not me—like Agag coming forth delicately, hoping that the bitterness of death was past. Yes, you. Remember, O man....

I was beginning to learn that when we encounter some "spiritual" truth in our *bodies*, it is brought home to us. We can meditate on suffering all day long, for example, but let us have migraines, and we know something we could not have known through merely mulling over the doctrine of suffering. We can meditate on love all day long, but let us kiss the one we long for, and we know immediately something we could not have known if we had thought about love for a thousand years. Nay—our very salvation came to us in the body of the incarnate God. "O generous love! that He who smote/In Man for man the foe,/The double agony in Man/For man should undergo," says Cardinal Newman's hymn.[35] The ashes effected something in me more than a smudge on my forehead. I had felt, if only for a moment, the thing that I wished most earnestly to be exempted from: death.

Lent proceeds to Palm Sunday, which along with Christmas and Easter is observed in many churches that do not otherwise follow the liturgical year. Here we see the "enactment" principle at work quite vividly. Palms are given to the people as a sign that we wish to be included among those who welcome the Lord as He comes into the Holy City.

Holy Week takes us through the events of this last week of the Lord's ministry. In many churches a service, which is not strictly liturgical, occurs on Wednesday night, and is called *Tenebrae*, darkness. It anticipates the darkness that is about to come down over the Lord and, indeed, over the whole earth in the events of the Passion, especially the Lord's descent into Hades. Candles are extinguished one by one as the Scriptures are read, until finally Psalm 51 is recited in complete blackness.

On Thursday of Holy Week the Last Supper is commemorated. The word *Maundy* which is given to this day, is thought to be derived from the Anglo-Saxon corruption of the Latin word *mandatum*, commandment, since it was at this supper that Jesus gave His new commandment, "that ye love one another as I have loved you."[36] This day actually marks the origin of the Eucharist, but since the day itself is so solemn, the Western Church eventually designated a day following Pentecost called *Corpus Christi* (the Body of Christ) on which thanks are offered for this gift.

At the liturgy on Maundy Thursday there occurs the washing of feet. In monasteries the abbot or prior himself kneels and washes the feet of the brothers. At the end of the liturgy the Sacrament is taken in procession from the high altar and deposited in a tabernacle on an "altar of repose" where vigil is kept. The whole rite brings home to us the disciples' sadness at the Lord's being taken away from them and what it is like for faith to attempt to remain true when apparently all is lost. Evangelicalism taught me to take these gospel events most seriously; the liturgical enactment of them brought them home to me. Centuries of Christian wisdom and practice were here to direct and give shape to my weak and helter-skelter resources of self-discipline and concentration.

On Good Friday no actual liturgy is celebrated. Various rites occur, including what is known as the "Mass of the Pre-sanctified," in which bread is used that has been previously consecrated.

At St. Mary's, as in many churches, the rite is somber to the point of being unbearable. At the beginning of the rite, the clergy enter, garbed only in white albs; no Eucharistic vestments are worn. As they reach the steps to the altar, they prostrate themselves at full length on the floor, face down. What other posture will answer to the mystery of this day?

During the solemnities a large wooden cross is brought to the steps of the altar and the people come, one by one, genuflecting three times en route to the cross, and then kiss its foot. It is very vivid and very physical. What is being enacted is what all believers cherish most earnestly, namely, that in this "sweetest wood and sweetest iron" lies our souls' salvation and that no love we can show will suffice. "When I Survey the Wondrous Cross," and "Beneath the Cross of Jesus," and "In the Cross of Christ I Glory," I had sung all my life, but I had never before done anything other than try my best to *think* about the cross. Here I was obliged to carry these sentiments into actual physical gestures. The act not only expresses something real, it gives force and clarity to it.

On Holy Saturday in most churches no rites occur until the end of the day when the highest feast of the Christian year is celebrated. It is the ancient Paschal Vigil, leading up to the First Mass of Easter.

It is a rite that seems to go back to the earliest years of the Church, perhaps even to years when the apostles were still alive. Toward the end of the day (afternoon, evening, very late evening, or, in some churches, just before dawn on Easter morning itself) the Christians assemble in the darkened church. The procession of clergy, servers, and choir assembles at the rear of the church, in darkness. Then fire is struck, from which the Paschal Candle is lighted. This is an immense candle, sometimes as tall as a man and several inches in diameter. There are affixed to the side of this candle five grains of incense, representing the five wounds of Christ. Then the deacon moves into the dark aisle with this single, flickering light. The procession follows him. Presently he stops. "The light of Christ!" he sings, and all the people respond singing, "Thanks be to God!" Again he proceeds, and again he stops. "The light of Christ!" this time on a higher note. "Thanks be to God!" we sing. Yet a third time it happens, on a higher note still. Then, from that candle tapers are lighted, and the flame is passed to all the people, who have been given unlighted candles.

Here is the church, glimmering now with this light from candles that are themselves almost perfect symbols of what Christ is, since a candle's light comes from its own self-giving.

Presently the deacon sings the *Exsultet*:

Rejoice now, heavenly hosts and choirs of angels,
and let your trumpets shout Salvation
for the victory of our mighty King.

Rejoice and sing now, all the round earth,
bright with a glorious splendor,
for darkness has been vanquished by our eternal King.

Rejoice and be glad now, Mother Church,
and let your holy courts, in radiant light,
resound with the praises of your people.

All you who stand near this marvelous and holy flame,
pray with me to God the Almighty
for the Grace to sing the worthy praise of this great light.

Scripture readings follow, tracing the history of Redemption: the Spirit of God moving on the face of the waters, Noah, the Red Sea, and other milestones leading to Christ.

Eventually comes the most blissful moment of all. Alone the priest sings, "Glory be to God on high!" Suddenly all the lights in the church blaze on, bells are jangled merrily by the servers, the organ thunders out its triumph, and Easter has begun! He is risen! He is risen! The First Mass of Easter!

The hymns for Easter are among the richest in the Church's treasury. "At the Lamb's high feast we sing/Praise to our victorious King.../Where the Paschal blood is poured,/Death's dark angel sheathes his sword.../Mighty victim from the sky,/Hell's fierce powers beneath thee lie..."[37] And Saint John Damascene's hymn, which hails "the queen of seasons, bright/With the day of splendor,/With the royal feast of feasts..."[38]

I grew up in a household and a tradition that loved the Resurrection of the Lord. Evangelicals felt that they were almost alone in defending the doctrine against the modernists and unbelievers. But here was the Church, celebrating this event with an amplitude of joy that finally seemed not only to answer to what I had loved and believed all along, but *unfurl* it for me. If we could blow horns at New Year's and wave flags on July 4 and have a picnic on Labor Day, why—oh why—were we denied celebration, ceremony, hilarity, and an extravagance of pageantry on this feast, next to which these mere national holidays were literally nothing—nothing at all? What religion was it that said to us, "No. Sit still. Or stand and sing, 'Up from the grave He arose.' But your main job is to *think* about the event and hear a sermon about it. Don't *do* anything."

I have often thought, in the years since those days at St. Mary's, "Oh, my own crowd, the wonderful evangelicals, with their love for the gospel and their zeal for God—how they would leap for joy if ever they returned to the ancient Church and thronged in by their hundreds and thousands, singing, praising, and bursting with pure joy at the discovery of the liturgy!"

PENTECOST

Forty days after Easter comes the Ascension, and then Pentecost, the birthday of the Church. The Sunday after Pentecost is one of the rare Sundays in the year when a doctrine as opposed to an event is celebrated. It is the Feast of the Holy Trinity. Then comes the very long "season of Pentecost" with as many as twenty-four weeks passing before Advent arrives again and the Christian year starts over.

There are other feasts of the Christian year, of course. In one sense the first should be the Annunciation, on March 25 (nine months before the Nativity), since this is where the earthly part of our Lord's life really started. This is a great feast. There is the Transfiguration on August 6. There is a number of feasts of the Virgin, since her life is the human life most intimately bound up in the mystery of Redemption.

REMEMBERING THE SAINTS

Then there are the saints' days. When I first came upon this practice, I thought perhaps it was a bad thing, since honor would be somewhat deflected from God alone if we set aside days to remember mere mortals like Paul, Peter, John, and Luke. But in the roster of saints we glimpse the court of heaven.

The title "saint" applies to all believers, of course, but in ancient usage it came to be applied to those who by virtue of being apostles, or martyrs, or very great teachers, or who by exhibiting some notable holiness of life were thought to be worthy of emulation and honor, just as in the secular calendar we honor men like Martin Luther King or Simon Bolivar.

On the Feast of Saint Michael and All Angels, the Church gives thanks for these great heavenly protectors whose ministry in our behalf we know so little about but who do seem, if we may believe the Bible, to be standing between us and infernal powers. At the Feast of All Saints, the Church remembers and gives thanks for all the faithful who have gone before us. One must remember that the saints are never worshiped. They are honored, and in some traditions their prayers are sought, not because Christ's intercessions in our behalf are not sufficient, but because He has made His whole Church one with His intercessory ministry, so that, just as we ask one another here below for prayers, so we call upon those who have gone ahead of us and who are more than ever part of this priestly Body of Christ.

Thus, as the letter to the Hebrews reminds us, we are surrounded with a great and awesome cloud of witnesses, men and women of whom the world was not worthy. Why, why will we most gladly set days aside to honor the fathers of our nation—Washington, Lincoln, Jefferson—but draw back in dismay from giving honor to the Fathers of our Faith? Believing what they taught is fine, but let us press on to the fullness of faith and give honor to whom honor is due. Let us once again build time around that which is eternal, Christ and His kingdom, and not merely around that which is passing away.

10

Envoi

The foregoing itinerary is not merely a private journey. Enough people are following a similar route to warrant our using the term "a movement in the Church." No one, of course, may seize on his own interests and shout, "This is what God is doing!" Nonetheless, something is causing thousands of stoutly loyal evangelical men and women to inquire into matters of the greatest antiquity and gravity. Observers who wish to find in the phenomenon only a taste for pomp and stained glass may be asked most earnestly to pause and attend.

A Family Matter

One point is worth pressing home: the "parties" to any discussion here are allies, not enemies. We all would wish to oppose cultishness and heterodoxy and to maintain the integrity of the gospel against all attempts to dilute or reshape it to fit modern categories.

The "catholic evangelicals," if we may describe them that way, are most eager to see the ancient Church roused and animated, speaking with a vigorous witness faithful to the gospel and teaching a spirituality vibrant with gospel life. On the other hand, they yearn to see evangelicalism, so energetic in so many ways, rooted once again in the mystery and authority of the Church understood as one, holy, catholic, and apostolic. They cannot believe that the Lord's words in Matthew 16:19

and 18:18 and in John 20:23, vesting his apostles with such august authority and unction, were idle, nor that Pentecost was the birthday merely of a clutter of conventicles, all jostling and jockeying and clamoring with a multitude of voices but no authority or unity.

I am aware of the matters that divide Christendom. Perhaps the most intractable of all are these questions of authority. But questions of piety and practice litter the history of Christendom as well. Sixty-five years ago, my parents were evangelical missionaries in Belgium, a region that would consider itself to have been Christian for a thousand years before anyone had heard of the Reformation. The procession of the Holy Blood at Bruges struck them as Tetzel's traffic in indulgences had struck Luther. It seemed only to thicken superstition rather than dispel it, as the gospel should do. Members of my immediate family have been missionaries in northern Canada, Ecuador, Colombia, and the Philippines, all regions which think of themselves as having been long since Christianized. But what of flagellantes, and marzipan corpses of Judas Iscariot, and local devotions that appear to crowd out altogether the worship of Christ, not to mention widespread ignorance of the holy Scriptures?

What of my Huguenot and Scottish ancestry? Will I side with Borgia popes, bejeweled cardinals, and haughty dukes against the valorous bands of believers crushed under inquisitions and Saint Bartholomew massacres?

To look back over Christian history is either to find oneself inflamed with renewed ardor for vengeance or to have one's heart broken, perhaps both. The cruelties and outrages that could be retailed for us by Christians from the England of Elizabeth I or the France of Louis XIV, or the Piedmont, or Scotland, or the England of the Stuarts, or the Massachusetts of the Puritans—who will reach the end of the recitation with his head high? Who will cast the first stone?

It is an irony of ironies that the *Church* has a history like this. It is bad enough in secular history to find wars, but what we also find in secular history is entente. We find peace concluded.

We may say all we will about the bad faith at work in secular diplomacy, but it remains true that countries which have warred with each other not only sign papers of peace, but actually enter into peace despite the immense issues that have set them at each other's throats. Does Greece still war with Persia? Does Rome still send its legions through Gaul? Does England still shell Boston's harbor? Do the American and Japanese fleets still fire on each other?

Little is gained by anyone's remaining fiercely loyal to his own history to the point of wishing to keep ancient flames of animosity alive. My ancestors were American revolutionaries against the crown of England, but I would be mad to fan anti-British sentiment in my children with tales of the war. Similarly, my ancestors fought under General Grant while my wife's fought under Lee. Shall we permit a small stream of poison to trickle along the border of our marriage?

A worthy pride in one's lineage both honors the bravery and integrity of that lineage and at the same time realizes that the kaleidoscope of history keeps reshuffling the pieces. Only pusillanimity and jingoism will strut and preen when they rake back through ancient conflicts. How doubly grotesque these attitudes appear in the Church.

When we pray for the unity of the Church, as we must do if we take our Lord's prayer in John 17 seriously, we only make our prayers difficult if we keep the memory of historic traumas alive in ourselves.

I myself am not one who looks to the committees in Geneva, however, to accomplish this unity. It is difficult for me to visualize the arrival of the Church's restoration on bureaucratic wings. (On the other hand, one does not want to be found droning, "Can any good thing come out of Geneva?" when the Holy Ghost is given to picking precisely such unpromising spots. And there will be places of honor, surely, in the Celestial Rose itself, for the intrepid souls who have sat uncomplainingly through decade after weary decade of ecumenical committee meetings.)

I cannot by myself, of course, untie the Gordian knot. I am aware of what the Orthodox church says in its case against the West, about *filioque* and Hellenism and Petrine infallibility. And I am aware of what the West replies about schism. I am aware of what Geneva, Zurich, Amsterdam, and Edinburgh say to Rome, and of what Luther says to Zwingli, and Calvin to Arminius, and Wesley to Whitefield, and J. N. Darby to all of us. Who does not stagger at the confusion?

What Can Be Done?

I have offered my undying homage to evangelicalism in this book. Insofar as evangelicalism wants to open the Scriptures to all people and to be faithful to the gospel and to love Jesus Christ the Lord, I am forever evangelical. To be fair, then, I recognize the question that may now be pressed on me: what, exactly, should evangelicalism do, in your view, if indeed the title of this book implies that it should do anything at all?

Certainly three actions would seem to present themselves for the most serious consideration.

First, there must be a return to the episcopate. Pastors need pastors. There is no independence among churches imagined in the New Testament, nor in the picture of things we get from the men who immediately succeeded the apostles and who had been taught by them. Teaching and ruling authority was vested in the *episkopoi*, not to grant power to a hierarchical elite, but so that unity and accountability might be realities in the Church. The office of bishop was pastoral as well as authoritative. It must be recalled by those who decry the episcopate that bishops assembled in council were the guardians of the Faith. The heresiarchs all believed the Scriptures, but they were interpreting it *wrongly*, said the Church. A doctrine of verbal inspiration was not invoked to guard the Faith. We may consult the early centuries if we think otherwise.

Second, there must be a return to the Eucharist as the focal point for Christian worship. The loss of its centrality has been a tragedy. The Lord's Table should be spread for His people at least weekly. The notion that this is somehow "too frequent" is a very late one, wholly at odds with the testimony of the faithful who return to this table week by week, and even day by day. Any dividing of things into Word *versus* Sacrament does violence both to the gospel of the incarnate Word and to us who have been invited to feed on the Body and Blood of Christ, not just to hear about it. "Take and eat," is our Lord's bidding to us, not "Take and understand."

Third, a return to the Christian year can only result in gain. Insofar as we keep the first day of the week as the day on which we gather, we acknowledge the principle of recurrent, disciplined marking and celebrating of the events of the gospel, since the first day is the day of the Resurrection. To move, with all the faithful everywhere, through Advent to the Nativity and thence to the Epiphany and the Presentation in the Temple and from there to Lent, Holy Week, the great Pasch, the Ascension, and the season of Pentecost is to have the Scriptures kept marvelously alive. To remember Paul and Peter, Timothy and Titus, Polycarp and Ignatius, and a host of others is to have one's imagination filled with gratitude for these forerunners in the Faith and to be *helped*. They have taught us, by their writings, by their lives, and by their deaths, and we are in their debt.

I might add two informal suggestions to these three specific measures. First, evangelicals might make a point of visiting the liturgy as it is celebrated in one or more of the "apostolic" churches—Roman, Anglican, or Orthodox—and of following as carefully as possible just what occurs. What is this most ancient and fruitful rite to which the Lord bids us in His very last act with His closest circle here on earth? Is it marginal to the Faith? What shape did it take so early in time, and is there any conceivable way of improving on that shape by perennial innovation?

Some warnings might accompany this particular suggestion. For one thing, a Christian accustomed either to informality in worship or to worship built mainly on verbal elements is going to be puzzled by some of what occurs. To some, the liturgy will seem elaborate or complicated, and they will ask where the simplicity of Christ is. They may recall for themselves that any ceremony in the world will need some explaining to a newcomer, and further, that this particular ceremony has been the resort of high and low, sage and dunderhead, king and peasant, for two thousand years now. That says something about it.

Furthermore, an evangelical, accustomed as he is to being surrounded by worshipers all of whom manifestly share not only his faith but also his way of expressing that faith, may find himself looking about at the people and asking whether they all understand and believe everything they should. This is the wrong approach, for two reasons. First the state of other people's faith is our business only if we are responsible for them; and second, faith is often scarcely recognizable across the lines that divide Christendom, so that C. S. Lewis, for example, smoking his pipe and drinking his beer at an Oxford pub, might not look like a Christian to a Christian and Missionary Alliance boy from Nebraska. A Sicilian peasant woman might have difficulty making a young woman from the Inter-Varsity group at Mount Holyoke understand that she is indeed born again. Heaven will be full of surprises, we all say blithely. Well, so is earth—and especially the Church on earth.

A corollary to the suggestion that evangelicals visit liturgical churches is that they *ask questions*. Lay people in the ancient traditions, however, are no match for evangelicals when it comes to having the answers at the tips of their tongues. Even the clergy in these traditions may appear less than articulate at times. But it is worth pursuing the search. Sooner or later some grizzled old priest will be found, or some old nun or laywoman, out of whose innermost being rivers of living water are flowing.

A final suggestion would be that an inquirer into these matters cannot go very far astray by doing some reading. A list of helpful books, ranging from popular to scholarly, follows this chapter.

I leave my task here, with this prayer:

> O Lord, we beseech thee, let thy continual pity cleanse and defend thy Church; and, because it cannot continue in safety without thy succour, preserve it evermore by thy help and goodness; through Jesus Christ our Lord. Amen.

For Further Reading

Bouyer, Louis. *Eucharist*. South Bend, Ind.: Notre Dame University Press, 1968. The Western authority on holy Communion.

Dix, Dom Gregory. *The Shape of the Liturgy*. London: Dacre Press, 1970. The classic Western work on how Christian worship developed.

Eusebius. *A History of the Church: From Christ to Constantine*. Trans. G. A. Williamson. Harmondsworth, Middlesex, England: Penguin, 1981. A fourth-century Christian historian writes about the Church from Pentecost to A.D. 325.

Field, Sister Anne. *From Darkness to Light*. Ann Arbor, Mich.: Servant, 1978. How one person became a Christian in the ancient church.

Florovsky, Georges. *Bible, Church, and Tradition*. Belmont, Mass.: Nordlund, 1972. Brilliant analysis of these three vehicles of faith.

Guardini, Romano. *The Church and the Catholic, and the Spirit of the Liturgy*. New York: Sheed and Ward, 1953. Virtually indispensable for an understanding of the genius of the liturgy.

Howard, Thomas. *The Liturgy Explained*. Wilton, Ct.: Morehouse-Barlow, 1981. An introduction to the liturgy written especially for newcomers.

Jungman, Josef A., S.J. *The Early Liturgy to the Time of Gregory the Great*. London: Darton, Longman, & Todd, 1976. Historical path of Christian worship.

Paul, Archbishop of Finland. *The Faith We Hold*. Trans. Marita Nykanen and Esther Williams. Crestwood, N. Y.: St. Vladimir Press, 1980. A well-written basic primer on the historic faith.

Schmemann, Alexander. *For the Life of the World*. Crestwood, N.Y.: St. Vladimir Press, 1973. A lucid and compelling explanation, for "outsiders," of the sacramentalist point of view.

Sparks, Jack, ed. *The Apostolic Fathers*. Nashville, Tenn.: Thomas Nelson, 1978. The earliest fathers of the church, immediately after the Apostles. Excellent notes.

Ware, Timothy. *The Orthodox Church*. Harmondsworth, Middlesex, England: Penguin, 1967. A moving history of the Eastern Church.

Webber, Robert. *Worship: Old and New*. Grand Rapids, Mich.: Zondervan, 1982. Popular written history of worship.

Notes

1. 1 Pet. 2:24; 2 Cor. 5:21
2. Is. 53:5; 1 John 1:7
3. John 3:7
4. Matt. 25:6
5. 1 Thess. 4:16
6. Matt. 25:41
7. Acts 1:8
8. 1 Pet. 3:15
9. 2 Cor. 11:3
10. 2 Tim. 3:16-17
11. Lancelot Andrewes, *The Private Devotions of Lancelot Andrewes (Preces Privatae)*, translated with an introduction and notes by F. E. Brightman (New York: Meridian Books, Inc., 1961). All quotations from Andrewes are taken from pp. 40–104 in the Meridian edition.
12. Luke 1:38
13. Luke 1:28
14. *The Hymnal of the Protestant Episcopal Church in the United States of America, 1940* (The Church Pension Fund, 1940), no. 195. Hereinafter referred to as *The Hymnal, 1940*.
15. Heb. 10:7
16. Louis Bouyer, *Eucharist*, trans. C. U. Quinn (South Bend, Ind.: Notre Dame University Press, 1968), pp. 29–134.
17. C. S. Lewis, *A Preface to Paradise Lost* (New York: Oxford University Press, 1970), p. 22.
18. Ibid., p. 21.
19. Ibid., p. 17.
20. 1 Cor. 11:25-26
21. John 6:32, 33, 51-56, 58

22. *Again*, vol. 6, no. 2 (June 1983) pp. 28–30. All the quotations on the following two pages are taken from this secondary source.

23. *The Hymnal, 1940*, nos. 199, 200.

24. See Gregory Dix, *The Shape of the Liturgy* (London: Dacre Press, 1970); Archdale A. King, *Liturgy of the Roman Church* (Milwaukee: The Bruce Publishing Co., 1957); J. D. Crichton, *Christian Celebration: The Mass* (London: Geoffrey Chapman, 1971); Josef A. Jungman, S.J., *The Early Liturgy to the Time of Gregory the Great* (London: Darton, Longman, & Todd, 1959).

25. This observation, and almost the whole of what follows in Chapter 8, has already appeared, much of it verbatim, in *The Liturgy Explained*, by Thomas Howard, (Wilton, Ct.: Morehouse-Barlow Co., 1981). The material is used with permission of the publisher.

26. Eph. 4:13

27. Rom. 16:16

28. Gal. 2:20; Col. 3:1; Rom. 6:4

29. Rom. 8:1

30. *The Hymnal, 1940*, no. 326.

31. *Saint Andrew Sunday Missal*, ed. Dom Gaspar LeFebvre, O.S.B. (Bruges, 1958), p. 69.

32. *The Hymnal, 1940*, no. 53.

33. Col. 1:24

34. Matt. 6:16

35. *The Hymnal, 1940*, no. 343.

36. John 15:12

37. *The Hymnal, 1940*, no. 89.

38. Ibid., no. 94.

Eucharist
Sacraments p. 108 - 128